CAMPAIGN 322

CAUDINE FORKS 321 BC

Rome's Humiliation in the Second Samnite War

NIC FIELDS

ILLUSTRATED BY SEÁN Ó'BRÓGÁIN

Series editor Nikolai Bogdanovic

OSPREY PUBLISHING
Bloomsbury Publishing Plc
PO Box 883, Oxford, OX1 9PL, UK
1385 Broadway, 5th Floor, New York, NY 10018, USA
E-mail: info@ospreypublishing.com
www.ospreypublishing.com

OSPREY is a trademark of Osprey Publishing Ltd

First published in Great Britain in 2021

A catalogue record for this book is available from the British Library.

ISBN: PB 9781472824905; eBook 9781472824936; ePDF 9781472824912;
XML 9781472824929

21 22 23 24 25   10 9 8 7 6 5 4 3 2 1

Maps by Bounford.com
3D BEVs by Paul Kime
Index by Fionbar Lyons
Typeset by PDQ Digital Media Solutions, Bungay, UK
Printed and bound in India by Replika Press Private Ltd.

MIX
Paper from
responsible sources
FSC® C016779
www.fsc.org

Artist's note

Readers may care to note that the original paintings from which the colour
plates in this book were prepared are available for private sale. All
reproduction copyright whatsoever is retained by the publishers. All
enquiries should be addressed to:

seanobrogain@yahoo.ie

The publishers regret that they can enter into no correspondence upon
this matter.

Osprey Publishing supports the Woodland Trust, the UK's leading woodland
conservation charity.

To find out more about our authors and books visit
www.ospreypublishing.com. Here you will find extracts, author
interviews, details of forthcoming events and the option to sign up for
our newsletter.

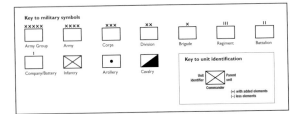

PREVIOUS PAGE
Arpaia, Campania, traditionally believed to be the site of the
Romans passing under the yoke following their entrapment and
subsequent surrender at the Caudine Forks. (Decan/Wikimedia
Commons/CC-BY-SA-4.0)

CONTENTS

Italy prior to the Second Samnite War

N

GRAECI Tribes or peoples

0   100 miles

0   100km

CENOMANI

VENETI

INSUBRES

Mediolanum   *Gallia*   Verona   *BOII*
     Cisalpina   Patavium

Cremona

TAURINI   *ANARES*   Placentia

     Parma

LIGURES   *FRINIATES*   Mutina

ILLYRIANS

Genoa

SENONES   Ariminium

Ligurian Sea

Pisae

AGER   Ancona
Arretium   *GALLICUS*

SABINI   Sentium

Populonia   Perusia   *PICENI*   Firmum Picenum

ETRUSCI   Volsinii   *UMBRI*

Vetulonia   Spoletium

Adriatic Sea

Cosa   Narnia

Tarquinii   *LATINS*

CARTHAGINIENSES   Veii

Aleria   Rome   *FRENTANI*   *APULINI*

Ostia   *SAMNITES*   Arpi

Antium   Luceria

Terracina   *VOLSCI*   Ausculum

Capua   Maloentum   *DAUNII*

Olbia   Neapolis   Venusia

SARDOS   Salernum   Brundisium

     Tarentum

Metapontum   *MESSAPII*

Paestum   *LUCANI*   Heraclea

Tyrrhenian Sea

Thurii

Carales

BRUTTII

CARTHAGINIENSES   Croton

     Locri

Messana

     Regium

CARTHAGINIENSES   *GRAECI*

Lilybaeum

Agrigentum

Gela   Syracuse

Carthage

CARTHAGINIENSES

ORIGINS OF THE CAMPAIGN

In its long history, the Roman Republic suffered many defeats, but none as shameful as that at the Caudine Forks (Lat. *Furcae Caudinae*, It. *Forche Caudine*), an enclosed upland valley at a disputed location not far from Caudium (modern Montesarchio) at the western reaches of ancient Samnium where the Apennine foothills meet the Campanian Plain. This was during the campaign season of 321 BC when the combined forces of two consular armies were surprised, surrounded and forced to surrender unconditionally. The captive Romans were not killed, enslaved or ransomed, but disarmed, forced to pass under the yoke and then set free. Let there be no doubt: Rome had suffered one of the most humiliating defeats.

Rome of the 4th century BC was little more than an Italic urban-based state vying with other Italic urban centres, communities and tribes of the Italian Peninsula that called it home too. The century was to be a crucial one for the fledgling Roman state, for in this mosaic of peoples, one opponent in particular lived in the mountainous lands to the south-east of Rome. They were the Samnites.

There were three lengthy, savage wars with the Samnites – who unquestionably ranked as one of archaic Rome's most formidable foes – that took place off and on from 343 BC to 290 BC. But it is the second of these conflicts that concerns our story. Rome had been at war with these rugged uplanders since 327 BC in what would turn out to be a long and bitter conflict that we now term the Second Samnite War. Though we should not look upon the Samnites as a single, monolithic entity, they were perfectly capable of mobilizing themselves and federating into a league when they needed to fight. The rising, rival Italic powers vied for supremacy in central and southern Italy, and their respective leaders were contemplating the conquest of the entire Italian Peninsula, or so we are led to believe.

Consequently, for the urban state of Rome it was a period of extraordinary energetic warring against the states and Italic peoples of central Italy, of an almost uninterrupted succession of annual campaigns. And truly so, for during the period 350 BC to 264 BC, Rome went to war yearly with the exception of six years: 347 BC, 344 BC, 328 BC, 288–287 BC and 285 BC (Harris 1986 [1979], pp. 256–57). By themselves the Samnites were sufficiently numerous and warlike to warrant paying special attention to. The Second Samnite War (327–304 BC) is described by Livy (books VII–X) in his inescapable but entertaining dramatic style. This conflict was particularly hard-fought, and the Roman army was to suffer a serious and humiliating reverse at the Caudine Forks, the focus of this monograph.

CHRONOLOGY

396 BC	Fall and annexation of the Etruscan urban state of Veii.
390 BC	Romans defeated at the Allia; Senonian Gauls sack Rome (387/386 BC according to Polybios).
384 BC	Dionysios I of Syracuse raids and plunders Etruscan coast.
381 BC	Latin urban state of Tusculum incorporated into the Roman state.
380 BC	Rome defeats the Latin urban state of Praeneste.
354 BC	Rome defeats the Latin urban state of Tibur.
	Treaty between Rome and Samnite League (350 BC according to Diodorus Siculus).
349 BC	Gauls and western Greeks threaten Latium by land and sea; Gauls defeated at the coastal Pomptinae Plain.
348 BC	Second treaty (as recorded by Polybios) between Carthage and Rome.
343–341 BC	First Samnite War (doubted by various scholars).
340–338 BC	Latin War.
338 BC	Latin League dissolved; Latin states (bar Tibur and Praeneste) absorbed into the Roman state.
	Roman maritime colony at Antium to guard Latium coast.
334 BC	Latin colony at Cales, northern Campania.
332 BC	Molossian *condottiere* Alexander of Epeiros defeats the Lucani near Paestum.
	Treaty between Rome and Alexander of Epeiros.
331 BC	Death of Alexander of Epeiros at the Battle of Pandosia.
329 BC	Roman maritime colony at the Volscian coastal town of Anxur (renamed Tarracina).
328 BC	Latin colony at Fregellae, northern Samnium.
327 BC	Romans introduce prorogation (Quintus Publilius Philo first proconsul).

326–304 BC	Second Samnite War.
323 BC	Death of Alexander the Great in Babylon.
321 BC	Romans humiliated at Caudine Forks; Rome surrenders Fregellae and Cales.
319 BC	Romans take Satricum on the Liris.
315 BC	Romans defeated at Lautulae; Aurunci revolt.
313 BC	Latin colonies at Suessa Aurunca and Saticula.
312 BC	Rome begins the construction of its first road, Via Appia (Rome–Capua).
311–308 BC	Etruscan–Umbrian War.
311 BC	Rome increases its number of legions from two to four.
309 BC	Roman victory at Longulae.
306 BC	Rome begins the construction of its second road, Via Valeria (Rome–Alba Fucens).
303 BC	Latin colony at the Aequian hill town of Alba Fucens.
299 BC	Latin colony at Nequinum (renamed Narnia), southern Umbria.

The Servian Wall (still visible outside and below Roma Stazione Termini) actually belongs to the period immediately after the sack of Rome by the Senonian Gauls, probably built between 378 BC and 350 BC. The wall ran for some 11km and enclosed an area of roughly 426 hectares. The accompanying ditch was 29.6m wide and 9m deep. A flat berm of about 7m lay between ditch and wall. With a basal width of 3.6m, the wall itself stood about 10m high in places, and consisted of two quite distinct building stones cut into individual blocks. One was a grey tufa or *capellaccio*, so named because it covers like a hat layers of pozzolana in the subsoil, which was too light and breakable to be suitable for walling on its own. The other was a yellowish tufa of better quality, Oscura tufo, which came from quarries near Veii (Isola Farnese), the Etruscan urban state that had been Rome's chief rival for supremacy in the Tiber valley until its annexation in 396 BC. (Salvatore Falco/Wikimedia Commons/ CC-SA-1.0)

The Samnite polities and their neighbours

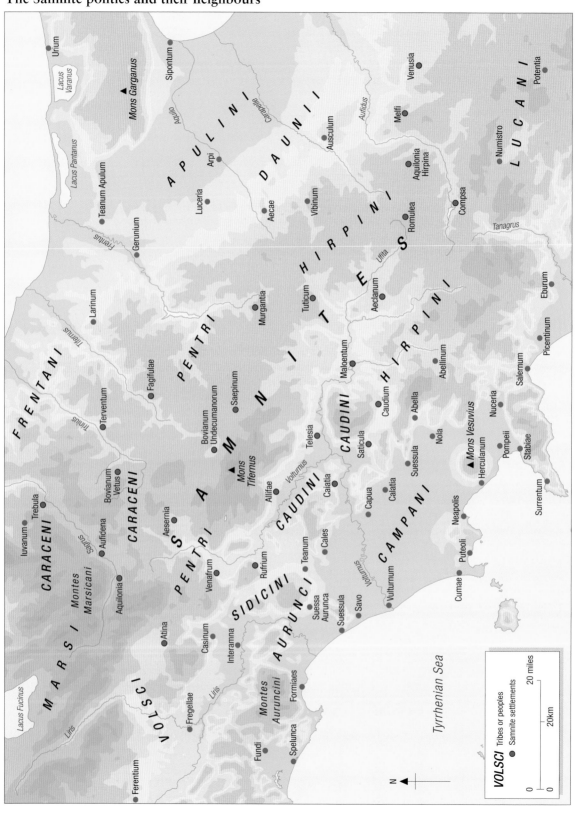

OPPOSING FORCES

THE SAMNITES

In the central and southern sections of the Apennines, most of the Italic peoples more or less shared a common but now extinct language known as Oscan, which belongs to what modern scholars refer to as the Osco-Umbrian branch of the Italic language family. As such, the Oscan tongue was, even with its many variants and dialects, linguistically akin to Latin, but had some distinctive characteristics and looks very different to the modern eye. The toponymic *safinim*, for instance, is widely regarded as the Oscan equivalent of the Latin *Samnium* (Salmon 2010 [1967], p. 28; Dench 1995, p. 200). The Oscan speakers themselves were divided into various ethnic groupings, the most important of which were the Samnites, who inhabited the mountainous region south-east of Rome down to the area behind Campania. At the time of their long, hard wars with the Romans, the Samnites banded themselves into a loose confederation traditionally known as the Samnite League (*civitas Samnitium*: Liv. 8.23.6). This league consisted of four distinct ethnic groupings each with its own territory – the Caudini, Hirpini, Pentri (Liv. 9.31.4, 22.61.11, 23.42.1, cf. Strab. 5.4.12) and Caraceni (Zonar. 8.5) – who can be roughly located in the Apennine zone extending from the River Sagrus (Sangro) in the north to the Aufidus (Ofanto) in the south. To these we should probably add the politically autonomous Frentani (Strab. 5.4.2, Ps.Skylax 15; cf. Polyb. 2.24.12, Liv. 9.45.16). But the creation of a Samnite League for the wars with Rome appears to suggest that 'Samnium', for want of a better term, was not a single cohesive region.

On the contrary, Samnium was a divided and dynamic social landscape responding to external threats and uniting for mutually beneficial political purposes. Samnium, such as it was, was a flexible region with continuous changing boundaries, and so caution must be applied to the notion of the monolithic 'Samnites'. The first reference to them is in Greek, Σαυνῖται/Saunìtai, and appears as one of the entries in the *Períplous* of Pseudo-Skylax, writing around 330 BC, which indicates that this people inhabited the littoral to the south of Campania:

> SAUNÌTAI. And to the Campanians there adjoin Saunìtai. And the coastal voyage of the Saunìtai is a day's half. (Ps.Skylax 11 Shipley)

To be sure, if it were not for the power struggle with Rome, the unification of the autonomous ethnic groupings who shared a common language

Warrior panoply and other personal items (Paestum, Museo Archeologico Nazionale di Paestum), necropoli del Gaudo, Tomba 164, dated to c. 380/370 BC. This belonged to a male aged 17 to 20 years of age. The greatest wealth of archaeological material for this period in Samnium has been recovered from the necropolis sites. The ubiquitous presence of weapons, helmets and armour in the male graves is an indicator that a warrior ethos was part of Oscan mentality, though there is a health warning: burial with war gear does not necessarily indicate that the deceased was a warrior, as the case of weapons buried with children clearly shows. (© Esther Carré)

might never have happened. What is more, this loose alliance was a marriage of convenience; the Samnites did not adopt an urban way of life, and as a result often formed new ethnic configurations. In the late 5th century BC a new Oscan-speaking people, the Lucani, emerged, possibly a southern offshoot from the Samnites (Strab. 6.1.3), and in the middle of the following century another Oscan-speaking people, the Bruttii, broke away from the Lucani in the toe of Italy.

The instability of the diverse Oscan language group was probably the product of population pressure, perhaps exacerbated by social and economic tensions caused by food shortages, droughts, crop failures and epidemics. We have no demographic records, but it seems clear from archaeological data that all over Italy the population expanded at the turn of the 3rd century BC, driving rustic communities in the increasing demand for resources to come to blows over land. Good arable land was in particularly short supply in the upland valleys of the central Apennines, rough and stony if picturesque and mountainous, and in the course of the 5th and 4th centuries BC the coastal settlements, many of them established by Greeks, found themselves exposed to the menace of the uplanders. Though they sustained themselves by a mixed economy of subsistence farming (emmer wheat, barley, lentils, peas and beans) and animal husbandry (manifesting itself most clearly in short-distance, high-frequency vertical transhumance), it seems warriors were the only vigorous crop that the Samnites grew naturally on their thin, stony soil. Furthermore, years of scrambling up and down scrubby mountainsides had made their bodies immensely strong, while the harsh environment of the rugged, chilly mountains and foothills of the Apennines fostered the skills of formidable fighters.

The 'others'

Much like Rome's other peninsula competitors, the Samnites are mostly pictured in Roman texts as barbarians (by which was meant uncivilized and uncultured), especially in narratives of the Samnite wars. It comes as little surprise, therefore, to find our Roman texts identifying them as the *hostis pertinacior*, 'most stubborn enemy' (Liv. 7.33.16), of Rome, considering them *gens opibus armisque valida*, 'a people powerful in arms and resources' (ibid. 7.29.2), and enumerate them among the *gentes fortissimae Italiae* (Plin. *HN* 3.11.106, cf. Sil. *Pun*. 10.314). This austere and martial image of the Samnites is linked, from the perspective of the geographical determinism of ancient deliberation, to the mountainous and wild nature of the country they inhabited (Bispham 2007, p. 180). The classic image of Samnite barbarism is Livy's description of the Samnites as *montani atque agrestes*, 'rough mountain folk' (9.13.7), who got their livelihood from plundering

Campanian red-figure neck amphora (Trieste, Museo di Storia ed Arte, inv. 5383), attributed to the Astarita Painter and dated to *c.* 340/330 BC. This is a libation scene with an Oscan warrior standing on the right, holding a spear and a shield, and wearing an Oscan-style tunic – a short garment with short sleeves and a rounded neckline, and either a straight, rounded or pointed hemline – and a crested helmet with three tall feathers. He faces a draped female figure, presumably his wife or mother, wearing local costume with her hair dressed in a *saccos*. In her right hand she holds a *phiale* to make a libation to the gods to ensure the warrior's safety and success in the coming campaign. (© Esther Carré)

their more prosperous and civilized city-dwelling neighbours settled in fertile coastal plains below. The passage in question refers to an episode during the summer of 320 BC, when the Roman army marched down the Adriatic coast towards Apulia (roughly equivalent to modern Puglia). As they approached the prosperous Apulian city of Arpi, they were welcomed by the locals because of the protection that they offered against Samnite raids, which clearly began to embrace more territory.

Though some scholars strongly refute this ethnic stereotyping of the Samnite as a rustic warrior and accordingly deconstruct it (e.g. Dench 1995), we should not discount the basis for the *impression* that the Samnites were formidable foes upon the field of battle and proved difficult opponents to Roman expansion in central Italy. Likewise, this stereotype, if that is what it is, has been reinforced by the iconic images of Oscan *guerrieri* depicted on Campanian and Apulian red-figure fine-ware. Of course, there is the argument that these depictions are largely filtered through Greek craftsmen working in regions peripheral to the Oscan heartlands. Yet the presence of Oscan interlopers in the fertile plains of Campania is known through archaeology (e.g. in Naples, Lomas 1996, p. 138), with representations of them appearing as markedly different from the other inhabitants, whose attire tends to be Greek.

To give one pictorial example to illustrate this point: on a Campanian red-figure hydria (New York, Metropolitan Museum of Art, inv. 01.8.12, *c.* 350/320 BC) a woman wearing full Oscan dress, who is attended by a young female servant in Greek dress, holds a *phiale* and an *oinochoe*, ceramic objects used for libations. The woman, most probably his wife, is greeting a returning horseman who is wearing an Oscan-style tunic and belt. The latter was a broad leather belt covered with bronze sheeting, fastened with ornamental hooks and occasionally elaborately embossed; the very symbol of his manhood. He also wears an Attic helmet adorned with two tall feathers. He carries on his left shoulder a *tropaion* with *clipeus* and 'streamer' attached. The latter is in fact an Oscan broad bronze belt, the spearhead having been thrust through its leather backing and bronze sheeting. These represent the spoils of victory, often bloodstained, and stripped from dead or captured enemy, a custom that goes back to Greek rule in Campania. An early 5th-century BC Campanian pointed amphora decorated in outline technique, apparently discovered at Chiusi (ancient Clusium) and now housed in the Vatican (inv. AB 14), depicts two Greeks riding white horses herding naked and bound prisoners of war before them. They are tied by their wrists to the reins near the horses' mouths. The horsemen, who are also naked apart from black ankle-high boots, carry two javelins, one over the left shoulder adorned with the bloody garments stripped from the prisoners. One horseman is bearded, the other clean-shaven. All four figures have their heads uncovered, and the victors appear to be making a slow trek home.

Given the apparent poverty of Samnium and the well-established tradition of settling new areas by force of arms, it was inevitable that the Samnites' need for land would someday prompt them to seize control of Capua (423 BC), one of the larger and most powerful urban-based states in central Italy, and of Cumae (421 BC), the northernmost Greek colony along the coast of western Italy. Eventually merging with the existing inhabitants of Campania to give rise to the Campani, Campanian society became a hybrid of the more urban culture of the Etruscans of the region – Strabo (5.4.3) speaks of a league of 12 Etruscan city-states in Campania headed by Capua – and the more bucolic culture of the Oscan invaders of the

Oscan broad bronze belt (Paestum, Museo Archeologico Nazionale di Paestum), Necropoli del Gaudo, Tomba 136, dated to *c.* 480/420 BC. This belonged to a male aged 25 to 30 years of age. Bronze plates fixed to a leather backing, Oscan belts were 7–12cm in breadth, 70–110cm in length and had a thickness of 0.5–1.5mm. They were usually fastened with two riveted hooks, which were inserted into corresponding holes. The belts served both a practical and aesthetic function. The appearance of elaborate *repoussé* or applied decoration on some belts indicates that they held important cultural meaning to Oscan warriors. Examination of these belts shows their value went beyond their actual monetary cost, as they were often repaired many times. Oscan belts are frequently depicted as a trophy hanging or pierced by a triumphant warrior's spear in south Italic tomb paintings and on red-figure vases. Some kind of symbolism has always been associated with warfare. This particular example is decorated with a scene (left) showing a mountain lion attacking a deer. (© Esther Carré)

Campanian red-figure hydria (Warsaw, Muzeum Narodowe w Warszawie, inv. 140351), attributed to the AV Group, dated *c.* 340/330 BC. A seated Oscan warrior with youth. Oscan men on Campanian (and Apulian) figured vases were conventionally depicted in warrior apparel, including Oscan broad bronze belts and triple-disc cuirasses: two upper discs with a third disc below the two and in a position midway between them and joined at the shoulders and at the sides. These vases are seen not only in Campania and Apulia, which had experienced Samnite incursions, but also at Caudium (modern Montesarchio) in the territory of the Oscan Caudini. (Artinpl/Wikimedia Commons/CC0 1.0)

5th and 4th centuries BC. Not long afterwards (410 BC), the Lucani took over Poseidonia (Liv. 4.36, Diod. Sic. 12.76, Strab. 5.4.13,), a Sybarite foundation of the early 6th century BC named after the god Poseidon, renaming it Paestum but maintaining the socio-political institutions set up by the original Greek colonists. A similar fate befell other Italiote (viz. Greek) *poleis* scattered along the south-eastern seaboard. In what was a dramatic cultural and ethnic change, these Oscan-speaking peoples from the Apennines imposed their language and culture upon all of southern Italy, except in the heel and in those coastal communities that remained firmly under Greek control.

Panoramic view of the Bay of Naples taken from Castello Sant Elmo, with Certosa di San Martino in the left foreground, and the distinctive twin peaks of Monte Vesuvio beyond. In the centre is Pizzofalcone, the site of the Greek *polis*. The history of Naples had its origins in the Greek colony at Parthenope. The settlement, founded in the early 7th century BC by the Greeks from nearby Cumae, took its name from Parthenope ('Maiden-voiced'), one of the sirens encountered by Odysseus and his crew (*Od.* 12.165–200 Lattimore, cf. Strab. 1.2.13, Ver. *G.* 4.564). (Wolfgang Moroder/Wikimedia Commons/ CC-BY-SA-3.0)

Palaeopolis (later Neapolis, modern Naples), for instance, took a different path. The Greek citizens voluntarily absorbed the incomers, and Strabo (5.4.7) records from the end of the 5th century BC the lists of δήμαρχοι/*dêmarchoi*, the chief magistrates, including both Greek and Oscan names, demonstrating that the Oscan-speaking migrants were given full citizen rights and that the socio-political elite had become mixed. Funerary inscriptions from chamber tombs unearthed in Naples corroborate Strabo's statement that the elite included people of Oscan descent, but Greek culture remained dominant in many areas of civil life, and Greek remained the predominant language.

It had been back in the 8th century BC when various communities from mainland Greece and the Aegean began to plant colonies along the Italian seaboard. The earliest, at Pithekoussai (Ischia), a small island off the Bay of Naples, was initially founded by Greeks from Euboia (Evvía) as a trading station and a staging post for Greek entrepreneurs on the coastal voyage north up the shin of Italy to Etruria. Palaeopolis itself, which probably was called Parthenope, had been colonized by nearby Greeks of Cumae. Other Greek settlements were to be founded on the fertile coastal plains of southern Italy and eastern Sicily so as to relieve population pressures back home, and to become sources of grain and other supplies for the mother cities. However, unlike colonies in the modern sense of that word, they were totally

Funerary art (Paestum, Museo Archeologico Nazionale di Paestum), Necropoli di Vannullo, Tomba 4, Lastra Ouest, dated *c.* 330/320 BC. A Lucanian horseman returns victorious from battle wearing a crested Attic helmet and triple-disc cuirass. He carries on his left shoulder a *tropaion*. The emblematic image of martial valour, a fundamental value for Oscan-speaking warriors, viz. the 'return of the warrior' motif, in which the warrior, loaded with the war gear of his vanquished foe, returns to his community and is greeted by his wife or mother, who holds a *phiale* and an *oinochoe*, objects used for libations to the gods. (© Nic Fields)

independent foundations and not subject to their mother cities, though they normally retained close cultural and sentimental links.

Crisis? What crisis?

Bone-poor, skilled only in hard toil and weapon-handling as these people apparently were, the Oscan warrior ethic encouraged wars of conquest, but in these fat lands the uplanders had established something like an ascendancy that abjured the memory of their warrior forefathers. Later, the erstwhile conquerors, who now formed the local aristocracy, readily became a spoil to the parent stock they left behind in the highlands. Capua, the leading urban state of Campania, had become a byword for wealth and luxury, and as Livy makes clear, the Campani had been softened by decades of comfort and opulence, which made them a poor match for the Samnites, a people *duratis usu armorum*, 'made hardy by the use of arms' (7.29.5). No doubt there was retaliation, but in violent exchanges of this kind the advantage lay with the men of the stony mountains, who were much tougher and more tenacious. Eventually, this would allow the Romans to exploit the worsening situation and support the Campani against their mountain kinsmen, an action that was to provoke the First Samnite War (343–341 BC). Campania was a productive and populous region, and neither side could afford to let the other get control of it: for the Romans it meant a good source of grain, and Rome was susceptible to local shortages (e.g. Liv. 2.52.1, 4.52.4–6).

The Liri, ancient Liris, at Canistro, Abruzzo. One of the principal rivers of central Italy, it winds its way from the central Apennines to enter the Tyrrhenian Sea just below Minturno, ancient Minturnae, under the name Garigliano. According to tradition, in 354 BC Rome signed a *foedus*, treaty, with the Samnites, designating the Liris as the frontier between the two peoples. As Rome pushed beyond the Liris, the treaty was broken and Samnite expanding ambitions and territorial interests were restricted, which made the path to war between the two unavoidable. (Marica Massaro/Wikimedia Commons/ CC-BY-SA-4.0)

LA SPADA DI SAN VITTORE

An iron sword blade, 41cm in length but minus its point, was unearthed in 2003 during excavations of a water cult sanctuary near San Vittore del Lazio, southern Lazio. The blade, which was deliberately 'killed' before being deposited, bears the intriguing inscription:

TR(ebios) · POMPONIO(S) · C(aius) · [F(ilius)] · [M]E · FECET · ROMA(i)
Trebios Pomponius, son of Caius, created me in Rome (*Revue épigraphie Latine* 90-2012)

The archaic nominative suggests a date of either the late 4th or early 3rd century BC, and this may well be the oldest known inscription of the name of Rome. Of interest also are the two Macedonian star decorations just to the left of the inscription. Also known as the Star of the Argeadai, it is a rayed solar symbol that was possibly the royal symbol of the Argead dynasty, the founders and rulers of the kingdom of Macedon from about 700 BC to 310 BC. However, representations of the symbol were widely used in Greek art, with hoplites depicted as bearing 16-pointed and eight-pointed starburst motifs on their armour and shields. The *Iliad*, too, describes the first cuirass of Achilles as being 'starry and elaborate' (16.134 Lattimore).

The sword itself, known as La Spada di San Vittore, is a La Tène B2 type common during the 4th century BC, but produced by a Roman swordsmith, rather than a sword looted from the corpse of a Gaulish foe, a gift from a Gaulish guest friend or an exotic item bought from a wandering merchant who had passed through Gallia Cisalpina. A typical La Tène sword of this period was somewhat slender, with a lenticular or diamond blade cross-section. Blades were generally parallel for much of their length, slowly curving to a very useful thrusting point. They were of high-quality iron capable of taking and holding an edge.

This brings us to Polybios' oft-quoted portrayal (2.33.3, cf. 30.8) of how Gaulish swords were made of such poor-quality metal that occasionally they bent double like a strigil on impact. This required the unfortunate owner to retire and stamp his blade back into shape with his foot before re-entering the fray. This view is contradicted by modern analysis of La Tène blades, which indicates they were well forged, with a good edge and great flexibility. Few of these blades descend to the pitiable quality described by Polybios. To be sure, Polybios' description of swords bending in combat is undoubtedly a gross exaggeration, for according to Philon of Byzantium, a contemporary of the Hannibalic wars, so as to test the excellence of their swords the Gauls would:

[G]rasp the hilt in the right hand and the end of the blade in the left; then laying it horizontally on their heads, they pull down at each end until [the ends] touch their shoulders. Next, they let go sharply, removing both hands. When released, it straightens itself out again and so resumes its original shape, without retaining a suspicion of a bend. Though they repeat this frequently, the swords remain straight. (Ph. *Bel.* 4.71)

Alongside these newer La Tène models, however, Greek-style swords would continue in use during the 3rd century BC, such as the *xiphos* complete with a Greek-style chapped scabbard and baldric sling.

On this point we might observe the mix of Greek equipment (Phrygian helmet, *knemides*, *xiphos*, *kopis*, *aspis*) and Celtic items (Montefortino helmet, bilobate long sword) illustrated in a series of gaily painted stucco reliefs. These life-sized representations decorate the interior of the late-4th or early 3rd century BC Tomb of the Reliefs (Tomba dei Rilievi) located in the Banditaccia necropolis of what was the Etruscan urban state of Caere (Cerveteri).

La Tène B2 type sword dated *c.* 300 BC from Münsingen-Rain necropolis, grave 138, Münsingen, Switzerland. (Sandstein/ Wikimedia Commons/CC-BY-SA-3.0)

Scale drawing of La Spada di San Vittore. (Drawing by F. Pittiglio; www.sanniti.info/spadavittore.html)

War, as the English philosopher Thomas Hobbes (1588–1679) was experiencing in the middle of the 17th century when the kingdom was being torn apart by a civil war, and those with personal experience know, is limitless death and destruction. By definition, it comprises uncontrollable, random events occurring in a vacuum when the laws and conventions that bind people and societies in peacetime no longer hold. According to the

Livian narrative, the Campani had come to Rome seeking aid against the Samnites, who were threatening them with death and destruction in the guise of war. The Senate had initially refused this request, noting that Rome already held a treaty with the Samnites, until the Campani, and specifically the citizens of Capua, surrendered themselves entirely to the Romans, an act known as *deditio* in Latin. This ploy evidently worked, and the Romans took up the war of the Campani against the Samnites, winning a number of victories, although they seemed more than happy to sign a treaty in 341 BC in order to extricate themselves from a war not of their making.

Various modern scholars have argued that much of the narrative was probably invented by Livy or his sources. Capua, as the most powerful urban-based state in Campania, certainly had the resources to resist the Samnites, and it seems unlikely that it was so hard-pressed that it felt the need to take this course of action. The *deditio* of the Capuans (and their fellow Campani), an extreme step usually performed by a defeated enemy who would be forever submitted to Rome like a client to their patron, is often argued to be a face-saving fabrication in order to explain why the Romans broke the treaty of 354 BC with the Samnites. This treaty had established the River Liris, which flows from Samnium into northern Campania, as the frontier between Roman and Samnite spheres of interest.

What we can deduce is that Rome was increasing its influence in southern Italy, and particularly Campania, which after all bordered Latium to the south, as part of its general expansion southwards during the course of the 4th century BC. The region, however, was already the focus of a number of peoples. Campania, as mentioned before, had a population of Oscan-speaking people, but it had also been settled by the Greeks as early as the 8th century BC. On top of that, it was under increasing threat from the Samnites. All in all, if there was such a thing as the First Samnite War, it was a reasonably minor undertaking in the grand scheme of things, another low-level conflict in a region already in a state of almost continuous low-level warfare.

If we choose to stay within the limits of what Livy (7.29-38) says happened, then the war started after the Samnites came down from the Apennines and harassed the communities of the Sidicini in the Volturnus valley, northern Campania. A Campanian force arrived to aid the Sidicini, only to be comprehensively defeated. This emboldened the Samnite raiders, who proceeded to occupy Monte Tifata, the highest peak in the long ridge which overlooked Capua. Though the raiding continued throughout this part of Campania during the first campaigning season of the war, Capua itself was beleaguered by the Samnites after another Campanian force was bested in the field. And so it was that Capua appealed to Rome for help against the Samnites.

In a league of their own

The mountainous Apennine uplands that run like a spine down much of Italy were inhabited by various Oscan tribes. The Umbri, Sabini and Aequi, who were Rome's more or less immediate upland neighbours, possessed small and loosely organized tribal polities, but towards the south-east the Samnites, a numerous people with a warlike reputation, were formed into a powerful, albeit principally defensive, league (Lat. *civitas Samnitium*, Gk. κοινὸν τῶν Σαυνῖτον/*koinòn tôn Sauniton*) capable of rallying sizeable and well-organized armies that drew from large swaths of the Samnite

Funerary art (Paestum, Museo Archeologico Nazionale di Paestum), Necropoli di Andriuolo, Tomba 58, Lastra Ouest, dated *c.* 350 BC. This Lucanian horseman bears a shield with a bronze rim and central grip. He wears a crested Attic helmet, bronze circular breastplate secured with cross straps and bronze greaves. He is armed with a stabbing spear and a *kopis* (Lat. *falcata*), which was much favoured by horsemen as it was capable of delivering a murderous downward cut (e.g. Diod. Sic. 17.33.7). As the Chalkidian form developed, the nasal guard tended to become smaller, only to disappear entirely, giving rise to the Attic style in which the only vestige of the nasal piece was an inverted V over the brow. The Attic helmet was extremely popular throughout the Italian Peninsula. Crests, if worn, were most often white, red-brown or black, from natural horsehair, but could be dyed. The end of this bushy crest hangs freely at the back of the helmet. (© Nic Fields)

uplands on a regular basis and did so against Rome for more than two generations. This implies that by the 4th century BC, they had coherent and effective forms of political, legal and administrative organization, and Polybios (2.24.20, cf. 2.24.12) tells us that even after the Samnite wars, the Samnites were still able to send 70,000 warriors and 7,000 horsemen to face the Gaulish invasion of 225 BC. Samnite inscriptions mention a *touto*, a term that seems to denote 'a people', roughly equivalent to Latin *populus* or Greek δῆμος/*dêmos*. The *touto* was governed by an elected magistrate known as the *meddiss túvtiks*, Latinized by ancient sources as the *meddix tuticus* (Lomas 2018, p. 163).

It is a mistake to view the Samnites as simply backward and unsophisticated. Our society is fundamentally urban as the ancient world never was, a difference obscured by our adoption of the Graeco-Roman equation of civilization with urban living; we, by and large, live in cities, and thus associate cities with high culture. On the contrary, the presence or absence of cities is not a yardstick for the attainment of civilization; urbanization is a red herring for much of Samnium (Bispham 2007, p. 201). The Samnites were industrial people, no more afraid to labour than to fight, as demonstrated by the sanctuary sites of considerable wealth and architectural sophistication that dotted the countryside, sometimes in close proximity to the fortified sites (variously called *urbes*, *oppida*, *castella* or hill-forts in ancient and modern sources) near which most of the population traditionally lived. The archaeological evidence suggests Samnite material culture was 'homespun' compared with that of contemporary Latium and Campania, yet it also reveals an upland society more dynamic, sophisticated and open to outside influences than previously thought.

So the Samnites were by no means uncivilized, and the cult places themselves undoubtedly had an important federal function in forging a connection between these scattered groups and in creating a common identity. Their socio-economic order and its institutions were clearly suited to the geography of the region, in a manner in which urban life, like that of Rome, was clearly not. At the macroscopic level, the harsh conflict with the Samnites, which dominated the Italian scene for a long time, could be viewed as one opposing lowland urbanized agriculturalists to upland raiding pastoralists. Livy (9.13.7–10) himself notes this tension. In this struggle, Rome clearly championed the interests and rallied the forces of the former, and this may well explain why urban states such as Capua threw their lot in with the Romans.

Yet (to repeat), in 354 BC (or 350 BC), according to the annalistic record, there seems to have been a treaty of friendship between Rome and the Samnites, which are now portrayed as a confederation of ethnic groupings that dominated the Apennine uplands of the interior of central Italy (Liv. 7.19.4, Diod. Sic. 16.45.8). This is the first appearance of the Samnites in Livy's narrative, and the historical reliability of this information has been, for various reasons, the object of different assessments. Generally speaking, non-Romans appear almost only

Apulian red-figure column krater (Trieste, Museo di Storia ed Arte, inv. S388), collection Baron Sartorio, attributed to the Dijon Painter and dated *c.* 370/360 BC. Unlike Attic vases, Apulian red-figure was not an export commodity, and most of the 10,000-plus known vases have been found within a hundred kilometres of where they were made. Italic people, rather than Italiotes, provided the principal market for the larger Apulian fine-ware. In this scene, we witness a seated woman who has offered a kantheros full of wine to a warrior (probably her husband or son) prior to his departure for war, or on his return from war. He wears a crested *pilos* helmet and an Oscan broad bronze belt. He is carrying a *clipeus* and two javelins. His Oscan-style tunic is richly patterned. The kantheros is in his right hand. (© Esther Carré)

when they interact with expanding Rome, and then they recede into the background as soon as the conquest proceeds elsewhere. In other words, their secondary role is essentially a passive one, at the receiving end of a violent conquest and all-encompassing acculturation. All that said, it is in any case interesting to note that from the very beginning the Samnites' history, like that of Rome, appears inextricably linked to war.

For the most part, the warfare in the Italian Peninsula was undoubtedly relatively low-level, amounting to nothing more than seasonal raiding expeditions seeking plunder and glory, or asserting the prowess or dominance of one group over its near neighbours, or quarrels between those same neighbours about damaged crops and stolen cattle. In this respect, Samnite armies were originally composed of armed groups led by local warlords, local 'big men' who shared a warrior ideology, which fostered the use of military muscle and economic exploitation to maintain status and accumulate resources. Then again, all of central Italy, and not just the non-urbanized Samnites, seem to have been dominated by powerful clans headed by chieftains who routinely promoted seasonal raiding campaigns. Seeking glory in combat and exerting a great fascination over their contemporaries, personal courage was obviously very important to these aristocratic warriors, and the bearing of arms may have been regarded as a potent symbol, first, of free manhood and, second, of power and wealth. This was a time when clan chieftains still rose and fell by the casual brutality of the sword, and it is extremely unlikely that many of them died in their beds.

Just prior to the period with which we are concerned, that is in the last quarter of the 5th century BC, the geographical range, frequency and scope of Samnite raids became much greater and started to threaten the coastal lowlands directly. These looting expeditions impacted farmsteads, as well as secondary urban centres and the occasional major ones, too, more than ever before.

Pontius' army

Then again, if we choose to stick with Livy, during the continuous wars with Rome there were significant organizational and tactical changes. Occasionally, it seems, the Samnites could adopt closed formations (Liv. 7.33.10), though their obvious successes in mountainous and difficult terrain confirm what Cicero implies (*Orat.* 2.80 [325]), that is to say, these doughty uplanders of the Apennine zone employed a flexible and open order of fighting, instead of relying upon, as did the Romans at the time, a close-packed phalanx.

It is possible, of course, that Cicero is referring to the *Samnitium* type of gladiator of his day (cf. Liv. 9.40.17), though Livy does describe the Samnites as forming *legiones*, legions, comprising cohorts of 400 men (8.30.11, 9.43.17, 10.40.6), and probably divided into *manipuli*, maniples, which the Romans would eventually adopt for their own army (Diod. Sic. 23.2.1, Zonar. 8.9.1, cf. Liv. 10.20.15). On the other hand, Livy (8.24.4) does attribute *legiones* to the Lucani and the Bruttii no less than to the Samnites, and thus may merely be using Roman terminology for the sake of clarity. Perhaps the best way to explain all this is to view a Samnite army as a composite one, with at least some of the participants seeing themselves

Apulian red-figure volute krater (Berlin, Antikensammlung Berlin, inv. 1984.42), attributed to the Painter of Copenhagen 4223, dated *c.* 330/320 BC. A deceased young man stands with his horse inside a funerary *naiskos* (limestone *naiskoi* remains have been found at Taranto). He appears relaxed, in a sculptural stance, holding the bridle of his horse. He wears bronze armour consisting of an Italo-Chalkidian helmet, adorned with a white crest, two white feathers and thin bronze wings, and a full-length muscle-corselet complete with shoulder pieces and *pteruges*. He also wears greaves and a pair of prick spurs. Hanging on the back wall of the small temple is an *aspis/clipeus*. (Bibi Saint-Pol/Wikimedia Commons/Public Domain)

as clansmen – in the sense that they were fighting in a body of men that had a consciousness of belonging to clans with ancient lineages and so fought under the command and leadership of a particular clan chieftain.

THE ROMANS

For those of us who study Rome, we have a tendency to view its social framework as being intimately attuned to the needs of war making. Accordingly, the evolution of the Roman state and its socio-political institutions has a definite military orientation, modern commentators tending to build up a picture of inexorability and invincibility. This may have been true of the late Republic and the centuries beyond, though of course we all recognize that Roman armies could be defeated, sometimes spectacularly so (e.g. Carrhae, Saltus Teutoburgiensis). It was quite the opposite during the age of kings and that of the early Republic, for there was no appreciable difference between the Romans and their central and southern Italian neighbours in military matters. All of this strongly suggests that we should give more consideration to the nature and scale of warfare between the Romans and their neighbours. After all, this was an age when rulers indulged in military adventures to satisfy a whim, to revenge a slight or an insult, or to collect booty.

In the time of kings

Rome's population and territory were not large, and the neighbours, which it raided and was in turn raided by on a regular basis during the summer

Funerary art (Paestum, Museo Archeologico Nazionale di Paestum), necropoli di Laghetto, Tomba 10, dated *c.* 330/320 BC. Two warriors stand opposed in combat, the so-called 'duel'. Both wear crested Attic helmets adorned with tall feathers, bronze greaves, Oscan broad bronze belts and loincloths. The one on the left wears a triple-disc cuirass. Both carry a single spear in their right hand, and a pair of javelins along with a shield in the left. The shield is unusual: apparently of wicker, rising to a central point, it is perhaps made of osiers, over which is shrunk wet hide. It does appear in other Paestum tomb paintings. (Carole Raddato/Wikimedia Commons/ CC-SA-BY-2.0)

THE TOMB OF THE FABII FRESCO FRAGMENT

Excavated in 1875, just outside the Porta Esquilina, which pierced the Servian Wall as it crossed the Esquiline Hill (65m) and survives today as the Arco di Gallieno, the fresco has been the centre of much scholarly debate, but it does seem likely that it belongs to the early decades of the 3rd century BC. It is argued that its theme is based upon episodes from the Second and Third Samnite wars.

In four horizontal registers, one above the other, the fresco depicts a siege of a stronghold and the awarding of military decorations. Painted inscriptions identify two central figures in the second and third registers. In the third and best-preserved register, a man labelled Q · FABIO(s), in ceremonial toga and tunic, extends an object in his hand to M · FAN, who wears bronze greaves, a loincloth and cloak. In the register above, the two figures appear again, and the man in greaves (and perhaps wearing an Attic helmet adorned with upright feathers) extends his right hand to the man wearing a toga, who holds a spear. The inscriptions are not so well preserved in this register, but it is possible to discern the second half of the name FANNIVS, making it probable that the first of the two figures, he in the ceremonial toga, is almost certainly Quintus Fabius Maximus Rullianus (d. 280 BC), triumphator in 295 BC, which was the fourth year of the Third Samnite War, when he won lasting fame for defeating a coalition of Etruscans, Samnites, Umbri and Senonian Gauls in the epic 'battle of nations' near Sentinum. This was his third triumph, having celebrated two previously (322 BC, 309 BC).

The career of Fabius Rullianus was certainly illustrious, having served as dictator (315 BC), five times consul (322 BC, 310 BC, 308 BC, 297 BC and 295 BC), and censor (304 BC). He first appears in the literary sources as *magister equitum* in 325 BC, when he won a daring victory against the Samnites at a place called Imbrinium, which is never heard of otherwise (Liv. 8.30.7–9). Ten years later, he successfully concluded the siege (a rare event, as will be discussed anon) against the Samnite stronghold of Saticula – perhaps one of the sieges depicted in the fresco – and then, less successfully, fighting at Lautulae. In 313 BC, he regained the Latin colony of Fregellae for Rome, and three years later overcame the Etruscans somewhere near Sutrium. He is one of the great heroes of the Second Samnite War.

The other figure in the fresco is probably Marcus Fannius; an argument can be made that the tomb actually belongs to the *gens* Fannii, but no members of this *gens* are mentioned in our literary sources prior to the 2nd century BC. Fannius is an Oscan name in origin, so it is likely that this character is actually a Samnite commander surrendering to Fabius Rullianus (La Rocca 1984). If true, then the fresco clearly commemorates the career of this Roman noble.

It has been suggested that the fresco is the work of Caius Fabius Pictor, a fellow member of the *gens* Fabii and a well-known artist (hence his cognomen) active in Rome at the turn of the 3rd century BC (Cic. *Tusc.* 1.11, Val. Max. 8.14.6, Plin. *HN* 35.19). He was the grandfather of the soldier historian Quintus Fabius Pictor, one of Livy's original sources and thus a collateral kinsman of Fabius Rullianus.

The Fabii were one of the most illustrious patrician *gentes* of Rome – they were apparently counted amongst the *gentes maioris* – holding the consulship 45 times during the Republic, as well as being prominent in the fields of literature and art. They are probably best known for their last stand near the River Cremera – the year was 477 BC – where the clan gathering of the Fabii with its 'three-hundred and six clansmen and companions' (Liv. 2.49.4) perished to a man (one half-grown boy had been left at home) during their private war against the marauding bands from Etruscan Veii (Liv. 2.49–50, Dio. Hal. *Ant. Rom.* 9.15–22, Ov. *Fast.* 2.195–242).

The Tomb of the Fabii, Necropoli dell'Esquilino, fresco fragment recovered from a wall of a chamber tomb, now housed in the Musei Capitolini (inv. S 1025). (Wikimedia Commons/ Public Domain)

months, were often barely a day's march from its own urban limits. By and large, the raiders swept down and passed on. On the other hand, if a neighbouring community was destroyed, usually by denying it the means of life via vandalism and theft, its fields were acquired by Rome and the conquered villagers often deported to the fledgling city and settled there as new citizens. This apparently happened to Ficana when the legendary fourth king, Ancus Marcius (traditionally dated 642–617 BC), took this riparian village sitting just 11 Roman miles (16.25km) down the Tiber (Liv. 1.33.3, Dio. Hal. *Ant. Rom.* 3.38.3).

Whatever the worth of the later annalistic tradition preserved in Livy and Dionysios of Halikarnassos, these threatened Latin hamlets and villages could often gain security by yielding before an attack, and the population might become the clients of the Roman king, *rex* (simply 'ruler'), or one of Rome's *gens*, an extended lineage group or clan, for want of a better modern term. Regarding the *gens* of Rome, there were recognized groups of both powerful and weak clans, *gentes*, power being increased through social bonds; that is, through the use of clients, *clientes*, or by bringing in outsiders as 'sword brothers', *suodales*. It may be useful to reflect on how the recourse to collective violence continued to be available to the *gentes* as a viable option even after the emergence of governments that in theory would have had a monopoly over these sorts of extramural activities. In other words, the armies of regal Rome were private in the sense they represented the war bands of powerful *gentes*. When called upon by the *rex*, clan chieftains presumably were supposed to provide contingents for the king's army. We may safely surmise these regal arrays once mustered were motley, to say the least.

Successful seasonal raids, whether occurring in the form of a state- or private-led activity, demonstrated a Roman king's or a clan chieftain's military competence, which was a principal requisite of good leadership. Brigandage was a way of life, accepted if not condoned, by society from the earliest of times, sometimes on behalf of the state and other times as a private enterprise (or as a combination of the two). 'It is according to nature', wrote the brilliant Aristotle, 'that the art of war ... should in a sense be a way of acquiring property' (*Pol.* 1256^{b}2–6). And so what we would recognize as a brigand raid was a typical 'war', a raid for booty – an all-embracing word covering cattle, metal, salt, female captives and whatever else could be lifted and carried away with relative ease. This was a world where the economy was dominated by moveable wealth and the exchange of prestige goods. In the socially embedded economy of archaic Rome (along with the rest of central Italy), the booty taken and redistributed oiled the cogs of the politics of the day (e.g. Liv. 1.54.4, 1.57.1). Furthermore, as well as learning the technique of plunder and pillage, the raid offered the opportunity for the younger warriors of the *gentes* to demonstrate their own prowess or skill, come to the attention of the clan elders and earn them advancement and other rewards.

The Roman kings (perhaps more than the seven legendary *reges* recorded by tradition) were often driven by the desire to conquer, and, as a result, internal disputes gave way to confrontations on a more extraneous scale. All the kings (barring the last *rex*, Tarquinius Superbus) increased the size, both in area and population, of Rome (Liv. 2.1.2). A word of caution is warranted, however, for despite the annalistic narratives about the conquests of the kings of Rome, there is no record or evidence of one major community permanently subjugating another *before* the 4th century BC. Even if the detailed narrative of Rome's expansion is of doubtful historicity, it is likely that by the end of the 6th century BC Roman territory had reached roughly the extent which the later annalistic tradition implies for the end of the regal period (traditionally dated 753–509 BC), with the last kings able to establish some form of hegemony over at least some of its subsidiary neighbouring communities in Latium. Another possibility was that peripheral neighbourhoods between two emerging states sharing a common boundary could be transferred from one to the other as a result of external conflict. Such was the fate of Fidenae, for instance, a small urban settlement in the Tiber valley that went back and forth between Rome and Veii several times (Forsythe 2005, pp. 242–46; Terrenato 2019, pp. 114–15). It must be said that Veii was unusually close to Rome even by the standards of densely urbanized Etruria and Latium, and the Tiber may have been the original frontier between the territory of Veii, which was probably larger, and that of Rome.

Joining Rome

A key feature of Rome's foreign policy during our period of study was to deal individually with allied communities, so as to minimize the risk of joint resistance. Yet membership of up-and-coming Rome was not simply a status that one did or did not possess. It was an aggregate of rights, duties and honours, which could be acquired separately and conferred by instalments. Those populations seen as ethnically and linguistically close to Rome were eventually admitted to full Roman citizenship. To those less close to Rome, a sort of half-citizenship, under Latin law, was sometimes offered, but they were liable for Roman military service.

On the sites of former settlements, or on land not yet settled, garrison colonies were planted: these were either Roman (*coloniae civium Romanorum*), in which case they were peopled with Roman citizens, usually around 200 to 300 settlers; or much larger Latin colonies (*coloniae Latinae*) of between 2,500 to 6,000 adult males drawn from allies or Romans who surrendered their citizenship (Lomas 2018, pp. 276–77, Table 9). The latter still had some autonomy, but fewer rights than the former – Latin colonists did not have voting rights – and were still expected to contribute sizeable contingents for Rome's armies when required. These contingents fought under their own officers and were entitled to a share of the booty. In both cases, Roman and Latin, the colonists elected their own magistrates, and passed their own laws. In this respect, it is important to observe that colonists were citizens of the colony first, and then enjoyed full or partial citizenship of Rome.

The decision to found a colony was formally taken by the Senate, with a significant role being played by the commander who had recently conquered the area where the colony was to be planted. Officials, including the relevant commander, were put in charge of selecting the precise location and organizing the new colony, carrying out foundation rituals, delineating boundaries, selecting colonists and allotting them farmland. In the latter case, the officials would divide the land, *ager publicus*, into small plots for *viritim* (literary 'man for man') distribution to the individual colonists. The actual 'bricks and mortar' of a colony was similar in layout to a military camp,

Rome and its near neighbours in Latium

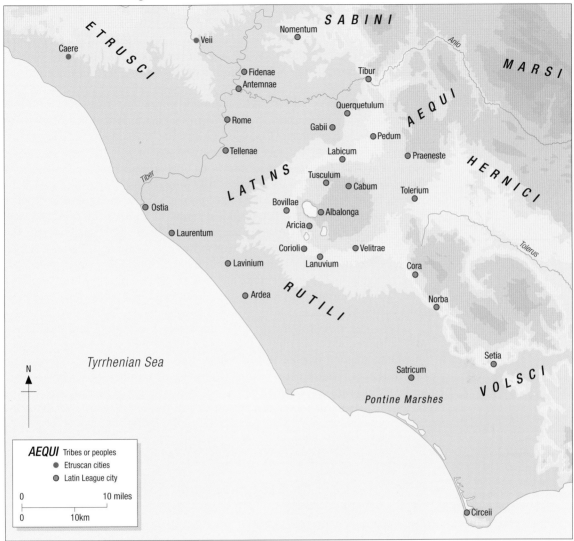

and most often built upon a 'virgin' or 'green-field' site. As well as being outposts of Roman military power, these colonies were also islands of Latin language and culture in hostile territory. Rightly does Cicero (*Leg. agr.* 2.73) observe that they were situated like fortresses across the Italian landscape. Another possible status was that of ally, *socus* (pl. *socii*), with or without treaties granting equal rights but still with an obligation to supply Rome with military manpower, which was to be a vital factor in Rome's ability to wage war continuously.

And so Rome began its long career of conquest and control through a common sense policy of extramural incorporation and integration, bit by bit absorbing all its nearby Latin rivals and gradually growing so as to bring other Italic peoples into its socio-political sphere by using a system which in effect was an arm's length relationship, thereby allowing Rome to dominate without getting directly involved in the day-to-day administration of its conquest and acquisitions. It proved a remarkably strong and stable system for excising Roman domination in Italy south of the Padus (Po), and it was to last for well over 200 years. The Social War – the war against the *socii*, which broke out in 91 BC, when many Italians revolted – forced Rome to accede to Italian demands for greater equality and to extend Roman citizenship. But all that was in the far distant future and lies beyond the remit of this book.

Around the year 390 BC, Rome directly controlled a territory of a few hundred square kilometres, but 50 years on this territory would grow to approximately 8,500km^2 (Cornell 1990, p. 367). As it did, so too did the scale of its conflicts. The fact that Rome demanded only military service, as opposed to tribute, provided an additional incentive to war, for the only way Rome could profit from its alliances was to make use of them in war. This development expanded the manpower pool available for service in Rome's armed forces beyond the geographical limits of Rome itself, and the year 338 BC marks a significant turning point in Rome's history. This was the year that brought the official integration of the Latins into Rome's armed forces, a profound development as it meant the archaic Roman army was no longer simply united by membership of a single community, but contained allied Latin contingents on a full-time basis, and became a more regional-based army.

There was still an appetite for ambuscades and raiding and plundering and slaughter, naturally, but there was a gradual shift from the archaic way of war to pitched battles, which required far greater military organization and resources. The choice of military response to capture and control of land and communities, or to protect territory from foreign incursion, was now to be a civic matter. As a consequence of this shift, the rough-and-ready, *gens-*

Italic Negau helmet (Trieste, Museo di Storia ed Arte) of bronze, 4th century BC. The Negau helmet was an indigenous Etruscan development, which first came into use during the 6th century BC, remaining virtually unchanged until the 4th or possibly 3rd centuries BC. The Negau represents the most common native Italic helmet, and archaeologically continues to be attested in Etruria and parts of central and southern Italy. In typology, it belongs to the pot helmet family. It was constructed out of bronze, and shaped in a tall, slightly bulbous angular bowl with a ridge that rises sharply towards the apex, providing two opposed surfaces designed to glance blows. The sheer volume of Negau helmets discovered indicates that it was probably the helmet of choice for most Italic warriors due to its simple, inexpensive design. (© Esther Carré)

Greek bell-shaped corselet and facing of *aspis* (Olympia, Museum of Archaeology, invs. B4985 and B5101), both of bronze, mid-6th century BC. This type of corselet took its name from the flange, which flared outwards below the waist like the mouth of a bell. The flanging helped to deflect incoming blows. The hammered sheet bronze for this type of corselet was generally 0.6–1.0mm thick, giving a weight of about 5kg. The breastplate overlapped the back plate, being secured by external hinge pins normally positioned on the left, shielded side. (© Nic Fields)

based war bands and their heroic chieftains were to be gradually replaced by a wider levy of all those adult males who could provide themselves with the appropriate war gear to fight on behalf of the Roman state. Up to that point, armies were small, and in comparison to what was to follow, inefficiently organized, poorly equipped and haphazardly supplied. Still, we must not get carried away, for the era when large Roman armies were effectively organized and uniformly equipped, well trained and harshly disciplined, and fully maintained by the state lay more than a couple of centuries in the future.

Urban-based army

Introduced as part of the Servian reforms – supposedly carried out in the late-regal period – the Roman legion had originally operated as a Greek-style phalanx, a densely packed block of citizens wealthy enough to outfit themselves with the full panoply of an armoured spearman, what the Greeks called a hoplite (though the Roman predilection to the Greek-style phalanx has been subjected to radical critiques).[1] The function of this armoured spearman had been the privilege only of those who owned a certain amount of wealth, poorer citizens serving either as auxiliaries or as servants. This required wealth must have been calculated in terms of property, cattle, goods, etc. since coinage was a very late arrival in Rome and *pecunia*, the Latin term for money, originally meant 'cattle' (cf. *pecus*). Even in the 4th century BC, Rome had only a rudimentary monetary economy lacking metallic currency, using instead *aes rude*, small cast copper-alloy ingots issued in standard weights and embossed with official stamps.

So by the time Rome was no longer just a hilltop village on the Tiber bank, yet still not very different in many ways from other communities of central Italy, the Roman way of war had changed from an agglomeration of numerous single combats to become an adaptation of hoplite warfare and the hoplite ideology of the decisive battle. Warriors are not soldiers. Both are killers, and both can be courageous, but disciplined soldiers value the group over the single heroic warrior. As such, they can operate en masse as a collective whole. Clan warfare, with its ancient allegiances

---

1 See, for instance, Armstrong 2016 (*War and Society in Early Rome*), pp. 111–26.

Attic helmet (London, British Museum, GR 1883.12-8.3), with a silver inlay depicting a satyr's head, late 5th century BC. With good ventilation, hearing and vision without sacrificing too much facial protection, this had been a very popular helmet in its original Chalkidian form, especially in southern Italy and Sicily. However, improved versions with a cranial ridge for better protection and hinged cheek guards for better ventilation appeared. The nasal guard also became smaller and disappeared entirely from some helmets, giving rise to the Attic style in which the only vestige of the nasal piece was an inverted V over the brow. (© Esther Carré)

of kinship, had given rise to confrontation and duels characterized by fervour and fury. For this reason, the advent of the Greek-style phalanx, with its armoured spearmen standing shoulder to shoulder, changed the very nature of combat: individualism had been ceded to collectivism, mobility traded for protection. 'Depersonalized' warfare had arrived, and the days of the brave whose fame derived from his individual prowess was over. Preliminary combats between individuals, a feature common to all warrior societies, did occasionally take place, such as the famous duel between the young Titus Manlius Torquatus and a Gaulish Goliath in 361 BC (Liv. 7.10.8–11): he went on to have a glorious career, thrice consul (347 BC, 344 BC, 340 BC) and thrice dictator (353 BC, 349 BC, 320 BC). But some commanders refused to put up with this; the same Manlius, now consul for a third and final time, had his son summarily beheaded after he had disobeyed his orders in a battle to duel with a Latin champion (Liv. 8.7.8–21). Battles had become directed efforts; the courageous no longer advanced unsupported, nor did cowards take flight.

All Roman citizens had full rights in private and public law, and were expected, if required, to serve in the army. Furthermore, like almost all the states in the ancient world, Republican Rome had an economy that was primarily agrarian: the vast majority of the population earned their livelihood from working the land which they owned. Accordingly, the Roman army was, in many respects, a militia whose recruits were expected to arm themselves at their own expense. The bulk of them would have been farmers who would have had little formal weapons drill, but who would probably have been expected to pick up the necessary skills as they went along. Roman legionaries were far from professional soldiers, but rather militiamen who, at the end of a summer's campaign, returned home to their farms. Consequently, despite the almost annual experience of warfare, their weapons proficiency and tactical manoeuvrability was limited.

Livy (1.42.4–43.8) and the Greek historian Dionysios of Halikarnassos (*Ant. Rom.* 4.15.6–19.4), both erudite rhetoricians and both writing in Rome during the reign of Augustus (27 BC–AD 14), attribute a major reform of Rome's socio-political and military organization to the popular king Servius Tullius (traditionally dated 578–534 BC). His first consideration was the creation of a state citizen army, and the most important point was to induce the adult male citizens to adequately arm themselves. So a census of all adult male citizens recorded the value of their property and divided them accordingly into five economic classes. Whether or not Servius actually existed, archaeological data and comparative studies do suggest that the Romans adopted the hoplite panoply around this time, so the annalistic

tradition, as presented by Livy and Dionysios of Halikarnassos, may be broadly accurate. Therefore, though the reform scarcely sprang fully fledged from the majestic head of Servius, it must be remembered that many of its principles rather than its details, which were elaborated only after years of gradual development, belong to this period.

If the account of Livy (1.43.1–7) is to be trusted and not completely rejected as a later invention, the Servian class I essentially fought with the panoply of the Greek hoplite, each man responsible for equipping himself with helmet, corselet and greaves (Gk. *knemides*, Lat. *ocreae*), all of bronze, and the *clipeus*; that is to say, the double-grip *aspis* carried by Greek hoplites. Weapons were long thrusting spear, or *hasta*, and sword. The minimum required wealth for membership of this class was 100,000 *asses*. As the classes descended, so did the amount of war gear a citizen was required to turn out with at the *dilectus*, annual muster.

In this manner, citizens of class II (minimum of 75,000 *asses*) equipped themselves similarly as class I, but were not expected to provide a corselet, while those of class III (minimum of 50,000 *asses*) could omit the greaves as well. Yet it does seem likely that the old Italic disc armour was still very much in circulation, and less well-off citizens probably wore this. It consisted of circular breast and back plates joined by a broad hinged band, which passes over the right shoulder, and secured into place by means of a harness in the form of leather cross straps.

Actual examples of these have been found in situ at the necropolis of Alfedena and that of Campovalano. Some 20–24cm in diameter, they are made of bronze backed with iron. The hinges and other attachments are also made of iron (Connolly 1998, pp. 101–02). Without doubt, Roman warriors wore a similar form of body armour (examples have been found outside Abruzzo), though the pectoral found in the Esquiline necropolis (Tomba 14) is rectangular in shape with incurving sides, just less than 20cm wide

LEFT: Italo-Chalkidian helmet (Karlsruhe, Badische Landesmuseum). With its hinged cheek guards and lack or near-lack of a nasal guard, the Italic version was a modified form of the Chalkidian helmet, though it may have been invented in southern Italy and Sicily (Snodgrass 1965, p. 34). The Chalkidian marked an improvement that addressed the drawbacks of the Corinthian form. An open-faced design allowed for greater range of vision and good ventilation without sacrificing too much facial protection, and the cut-outs to the sides of the helmet meant far less impeded hearing; both important factors for soldiers on a battlefield and hence its popularity. **RIGHT:** Etruscan bronze votive of a warrior (London, British Museum, inv. 1847.1101.5), found on Monte Falterona in the Apennines, dated *c.* 420/400 BC. The hinged cheek guards of his helmet are upturned. (Left – © Esther Carré; Right – Paul Hudson/ Flickr/CC-BY-SA-2.0)

Detail on Sarcofago delle Amazzoni (Firenze, Museo Archeologico Nazionale di Firenze), dated 350/325 BC. Discovered in 1869 in a grave not far from Tarquinia (formerly Corneto), ancient Tarquinii (Lat.) or Tarch(u)na (Etr.). Tempera painting on a marble sarcophagus with lively scenes depicting the clash between the Greeks and the Amazons (Amazonomachia). The warrior wears a *linôthorax*, linen 'stiff shirt' cuirass, which was constructed from several layers of linen glued together to make body armour about 5mm thick. The example depicted here is shown reinforced with lamellar plates. The three advantages of the *linôthorax* were its cost, lightness and flexibility. His helmet is an Apulo-Corinthian and he wears greaves. He is armed with a *hasta* and *xiphos*, and bears a *clipeus*. (Sailko/Wikimedia Commons/CC-BY-SA-3.0)

and just more than 20cm in length. The shorter sides are pierced with holes for the stitching of a leather backing and the attachment of leather straps to hold the pectoral in place. It protected only the upper chest. This armour compares well with Polybios' description of the καρδιοφφύλαξ/*kardiophylax* (Lat. *pectorale*) worn by the *hastati* of his day. Made of bronze, this pectoral was 'a span (σπιθαμή) square' (Polyb. 6.23.14); that is, 23cm each side.

Though of limited protection, the importance of armour to those who fight at close quarters can hardly be overstressed. Apart from the obvious protection it offers, it lends confidence to the wearer, and confidence in combat is always extremely important. As Colonel Ardant du Picq (1821–70), the French infantry officer and military theorist who wrote on the importance of morale in battle to the individual soldier, rightly noted: 'Armour, in diminishing the material effect that can be suffered, diminishes the dominating morale effect of fear' (1903 [1946], p. 119).

On the other hand, to balance the absence of body armour, if that was the case, classes II and III did carry the oval *scutum* instead of the circular, bowl-shaped *clipeus*. This was a body shield, Italic in origin. Throughout the history of human aggression, the use of spear and shield has been inextricably linked, and with this new style of spear–shield warfare the weapon par excellence of at least the spearmen of classes I to III was the *hasta*, the long thrusting spear. Finally, classes IV and V (minimum of 25,000 and 11,000 *asses* respectively) were armed as skirmishers, the last class perhaps carrying nothing more than a sling, although Dionysios of Halikarnassos allows them a javelin (*saunion*) too (*Ant. Rom.* 4.17.2).

Generally speaking, the historical process is a rather messy business and often works itself out in total defiance of neat, sound schemes. Thus, it has been suggested there were in fact two stages of development here: first, a single undifferentiated class, *classis*, of those who possessed the minimum qualification to serve as heavily armoured spearmen with all the rest named *infra classem*, 'below the class' (so the elder Cato in Fest. 100L, Gell. *NA* 6.13), which refers to those whose census rating was below 100,000 *asses* (though Aulus Gellius says 125,000, and the late lexicographer Festus 120,000); then the later classes being slowly introduced at later dates – possibly as late as the 4th century BC. This hypothesis would certainly better reflect a period when the art of war in the Italian Peninsula was in the melting pot.

More important was the later subdivision of these five classes into centuries, *centuriae*: in each class half the centuries were made up of elder men (*seniores*, those whose ages ranged from 47 to 60), obviously more suitable for garrison duty, and half of younger men (*iuniores*, those aged from 17 to 46). The centuries in each class were unequal in number, as the state naturally drew more heavily upon the well-equipped wealthier men than on those lower down the property ladder. Thus, class I contained 80 *centuriae*; classes II, III and IV 20 each; and class V 30. Below them were five *centuriae* of unarmed men, four of artisans and one of *proletarii*, whose property was too little to justify enrolment in class V. Known as *capite censi*, 'counted by heads',

Italo-Chalkidian helmet (Malibu, J. Paul Getty Museum, Villa Collection, inv. 93.AC.27) of bronze, dated *c.* 350/300 BC, typical of many discovered in Samnite tombs. Details added include eyebrows, hair curls over a diadem and hinged cheek guards adorned with side locks and a striding animal. The crowning griffin's head, wings and spiralled feather holders were added last. This type of helmet appears to have evolved from the Corinthian helmet, with Greek armourers overcoming some of the inherent deficiencies in the Corinthian design by creating cut-outs for the ears and enlarging the face opening in the Chalkidian variant. These improvements made for a lighter helmet with greater vision and hearing, while still providing good protection. (J. Paul Getty Musuem/ CC-BY-SA-4.0)

these men were simply counted and had no military obligations, no political rights and were not taxed. In other words, poverty – curiously perhaps to us moderns – freed men from conscription. At the other extreme were those who served on horseback, the sons of the well-to-do, making up 18 *centuriae*, which took precedence over the *centuriae* of the other five classes.

Servius Tullius was perhaps the first among Rome's rulers to realize that the days of individual combat and aristocratic heroics should come to an end. In doing so he had conceived of a state organized exclusively for war. Whether or not he succeeded with his designs is a matter of fierce scholarly debate. Still, later under the mature Republic, we do know that the Servian system would provide the basis of the *comitia centuriata*, the 'assembly in centuries', at which all adult male Roman citizens with the right to vote did so to declare war or accept peace, to elect the consuls, praetors and censors, the senior magistrates (i.e. offices with *imperium*) of Rome and to judge capital cases. Gathering on the *campus Martius*, the Field of Mars, a sizeable open area located on the northern fringe of the city (reflecting the ancient taboo of bringing the army into Rome), and enveloped by a bend of the Tiber, its structure exemplified the ideal of a militia in battle array, men voting and fighting together in the same units.

As opposed to the 'arithmetic equality' of democratic Athens, the *comitia centuriata* operated on a 'timocratic principle', the common idea whereby the property-owning classes lived in a 'stakeholder' society, where political rights are defined by military obligations, which in turn spring from the need to defend property; property itself gives the financial means to engage in that defence. Those who have property, and thus a stake and a role in the defence of society, are considered more likely to take sensible decisions about how the state is run. The richer you are, the truer this becomes, and conversely, having nothing to lose will make you irresponsible. The timocratic principle meant that only those who could afford arms could vote, which meant the *comitia centuriata* was in effect an assembly of property-owners-cum-citizen-soldiers. While they both tend to agree, in broad terms, on the basic form and organization, strangely enough the Servian army of Livy and Dionysios of Halikarnassos does not appear in their respective campaign or battle accounts.

THE SOURCE: TITUS LIVIUS

Before we consider the humiliating tragedy at the Caudine Forks, we need to examine our most complete surviving source for this ill-starred Roman adventure. During the long and relatively peaceful reign of Augustus, Titus Livius (d. AD 17) of Patavium (Padua, Padova) laboured hard and long over what was to become, in 142 books (35 of which are still extant), his monumental, all-encompassing history of Rome and the Roman people from the foundation of the city down to 9 BC. Yet tucked away deep within *Ab Urbe Condita Libri*, 'Books from the Foundation of the City', is a short story easily overlooked or forgotten by the reader. There, in a single passage, Livy illustrates the grave danger of half measures and middle roads in war. His message is clear: Romans, take heed of the lessons learned at the Caudine Forks.

In the course of his narrative of the Second Samnite War, Livy laments the unreliability of the historical record for this period in a lengthy passage (8.40.3–6), in which he states his belief that the record of this period has been falsified for the greater glory of the leading *gentes* of Rome by such means as funeral orations, fictitious inscriptions on portrait busts of their forbearers and other dodgy claims to illustrious achievements and brave deeds. He further laments that no reliable or contemporary extended narratives for the period exist. Fact, fable and fiction are but the two ends and the middle of a scale which ranges through all the intervening shades of grey. What is fact, fable or fiction in Livy's narrative covering the early history of Rome is a tantalizing question that has been – and still is – a matter of much academic debate and dispute. There can be no conclusive answer, and the problem has been discussed at great length by Gary Miles (1997 [1995]).

The history of at least the first two centuries of the Republic, when Rome was entirely involved in the struggle with its near neighbours – and with some distant ones – is particularly prone to doubts owing to the absence of any official records apart from the various *fasti*, the calendars of the days allowed for official business, which listed only the magistrates for each year and state occasions such as the triumphs. Livy had to rely on earlier sources such as Quintus Fabius Pictor – he calls him 'our oldest authority' (1.44.2) – the first native historian of Rome, a patrician senator (and likely hellenophile, given his choice of written language, Greek, and genre) who took an active part in the war with Hannibal.[2] This left a

---

2   For the Samnite wars, Livy mentions Fabius Pictor on two occasions (8.30.8, 10.37.13).

sizeable gap after the traditional date of the foundation of the Republic, 509 BC. When the sources were incomplete, there was a tendency on Livy's part to flesh out the barebones of available data from local legend and homely hearsay, helped by his fertile imagination. When all else failed, Livy's aim was to write a cracking good story.

So the story of archaic Rome appears to be a confection of oral traditions, confused folk memories, hoary myths, dubious romantic fiction and outright lies. Still, whatever contextual challenges exist with this incident, Livy did not invent his account of the Roman military defeat at the Caudine Forks or its immediate aftermath. Cicero, for example, makes mention of the incident in his *De officiis*. Here Cicero writes:

Bronze bust of Titus Livius (Warsaw, Muzeum Narodowe w Warszawie, inv. 164751), by the Paduan sculptor Andrea Briosco, detto il Riccio, (d.1532). Despite the fame of his *Ab Urbe Condita Libri*, few details are known of the author's life apart from his birth and death in Patavium (Padua). An epitaph (*ILS* 2919) from that city commemorating a Titus Livius, his two sons and a wife is probably the historian's. The literary sources concerning the Caudine Forks are unfortunately scarce, Livy being the only extant literary source to give a continuous account of the Second Samnite War, and there are moments when reading his narrative on the battle that feel as if he occupies the sweet spot between fact and fiction. (Dariusz Kaczmarzyk/Wikimedia Commons/CC0 1.0)

The Caudine Forks – possible locations

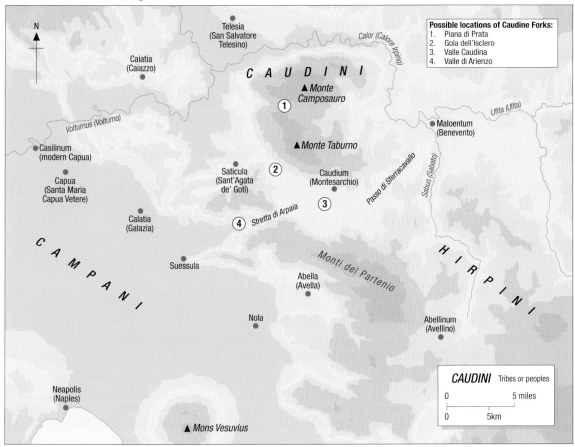

At vero T. Veturius et Sp. Postumius cum iterunt consules essent, quia, cum
male pugnatum apud Caudium esset, legionibus nostris sub iugum missis
pacem cum Samnitibus feceran, deditii sunt iis; iniussu enim populi senatusque
fecerant.

And indeed, Titus Veturius and Spurius Postumius, when they were consuls
for the second time, were handed over to the Samnites because they had signed
a peace treaty with them after the Romans were defeated at Caudium and the
legions sent under the yoke – for the consuls had done this without the
approval of the Roman Senate and people. (Off. 3.109)

Indications derived from other Graeco-Roman texts offer little help; much
like Cicero, none is sufficiently specific with regard to what actually came to
pass in that fatal upland valley. Here are some samples:

legionibus Romanis apud furcas Caudinas inclusis …
Roman soldiers captured at the Caudine Forks … (Val. Max. 7.2.14)

Cluso per insidias intra eum saltum exercitu, unde non posset evadere …
The Roman army having been entrapped by an ambush in that defile and
being able to escape … (Flor. 1.11.10, cf. 1.34.7)

in locis iniquis circumvallati ...
in an unlucky situation were surrounded ... (Gell. *NA* 17.21.36)

ubi cum Veturium et Postumium consules omnesque copias Romanorum
angustiis locorum armisque clausissent.
their armed forces blocked the passes and shut in the consuls Veturius and
Postumius and all the Roman troops. (Oros. 3.15.3)

καὶ τότε καταφρονήσουτες οἱ Ῥωμαῖοι καὶ ὑπὸ Ποντίου τοῖ Σαυνίτου
κατακλεισθέντες εἰς ἀνεξόδους δυσχωρίας ...
and having been hemmed in by Pontius the Samnite into a difficult position
from which to escape was impossible, when they were now on the point of
perishing from famine ... (Dio. Hal. *Ant. Rom.* 16.1.4)

ἐς γὰρ στενώτατον χῶρον τούτους συγκλείσαντες ...
and having shut the Romans up in a defile where they were oppressed by
hunger ... (App. *Sam.* 4.2)

τὸ στρατόπεδον αὐτῶν ἐζώγρησαν καὶ πάντας ὑπὸ τὸν ζυγὸν ὑπήγαγον.
captured alive the entire Roman army, and sent them all under the yoke. (Dio
8.36.10)

To return to our main source of information: Livy. He was a great patriot
and it showed up in his writings, but even he could not minimize the
Roman shame after the disgraceful performance of the two consuls at the
Caudine Forks.

Naturally, there are times when you feel you could do without the tedious,
interminable speeches that Livy inevitably invents for the dramatis personae
in any major action. Likewise, you can easily criticize Livy for his treatment of
military history whereby much emphasis is given to the emotional reactions
of the dramatis personae, all described in epic and poetic terms, with slight
attention to topography or tactics. However, it is important to remember
that for the Greeks and Romans, history was a branch of literature intended
to entertain as well as inform and inspire. In this regard, therefore, Livy was
not a historian in the modern sense of the word, for his historiographical
project was less the comprehension of the past than the political education
and moral edification of his contemporaries. As a result, although obviously
engaging, well-written and very likely well-researched (after all, this was his
life's work), there seems to have been no way for Livy to have known for
sure many of the details included in his *opus magnus*. His was criticized by a
contemporary historian, Caius Asinius Pollio, a Caesarian partisan who had
fought in the civil wars, for his *Patavinitas*, 'Paduaness' (Quintinian 1.5.56,
8.1.3), the provincial smack of his native Patavium to typify Livy's writing.
His arc was home-grown.

By our standards the patriotic Livy may be a rotten historian, the historical
substance of his accounts falling under the shadow of uncertainty cast by the
nonexistent documentary record of Rome in its beginnings, but he was for
sure a good journalist who liked nothing better than a good yarn. Written
at a time when Rome itself was still shocked and riven by anarchy, in many
respects the first ten books of his great saga harp back to the so-called golden
years of Rome and allowed the Romans of his day to wallow in their own

history and traditions. However, even if we must suspect that Livy indulges in a measure of bardic licence, his *Ab Urbe Condita Libri* is not a flat-footed lament for departed glory and certainly has its uses as long as it is treated with wary but sympathetic caution.

Having said this, there still remains the cogent argument that Livy had no first-hand military experience, unlike Polybios, for instance, a singularly inspired individual who had considerable practical experience in war. This undoubtedly carries more than a large pinch of truth, for he does certainly appear to be uninformed when it comes to military matters, particularly in regard to military equipment. For instance, Livy describes the form of the Samnite shield as this: 'the upper part was quite broad where it protected the breast and shoulders and had a smooth rim, while the base was rather tapering, for easy handling' (9.40.2–3). This is certainly at odds with the archaeological record. Yet in the same passage the author does describe the Samnites as using *spongia* as *pectori tegumentum* and wearing crested helmets (9.40.3), which do appear in the archaeological record. The Latin *spongia* is literally 'sponge', while *pectori tegumentum* is 'protection for the chest'. In other words, Livy is probably referring to the triple-disc bi-valve cuirass. Likewise, the Samnite helmet was made distinctive by a variety of ornamental

Flauius Blondus

Portrait of Flavio Biondo da Forlì (Lat. Flavius Blondus), illustrated in Paolo Giovio, *Elogia Virorum Literis Illustrium* (Basel, 1577). The Italian Renaissance humanist historian was one of the first historians to use a tripartite division of history (ancient, medieval, modern) and is known as one of the first archaeologists. His *Italia Illustrata* (1451) is the geography, based on the author's personal travels, and history of Italy's 18 *regiones* of antiquity. Unlike medieval geographers, who tended to focus on their own backyard, Biondo, taking Strabo as his role model, reinstated the rational idea of *Italy* to include the whole peninsula. Through the tool of topography, he linked antiquity with modern times to throw some light – *illustrare* (hence the title) – onto two millennia of Italian history. As a result, he was the first to offer a crisp and well-informed study of the Caudine Forks by relating the ancient topography to the surviving accounts. (Wikimedia Commons/Public Domain)

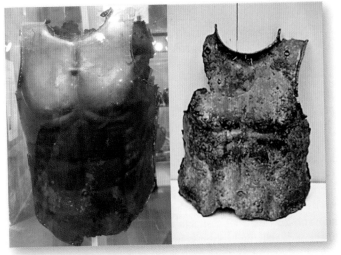

details, such as horsehair crests and upright feathers. Even so, it must be said that no amount of arms or armour will provide the same level of detail as that contained in the literary sources.

Though the supposition, solidly argued and unassailably rooted, that the fighting, however much there actually was, did take place in the upland valley between Arienzo and Arpaia (the traditional location for Caudine Forks), there still remains the unpalatable truth that Livy, or his annalistic source, did not actually visit the Caudine Forks to walk and examine the terrain. Livy describes the ambush:

LEFT: Full-length Etruscan muscle-corselet (Orvieto, Museo Archeologico Nazionale di Orvieto) of bronze, from the Tomba del Guerriero near Porano, 4th century BC. The grey colouring suggests the plate was originally tinned or silvered. **RIGHT:** Short Italiote muscle-corselet (London, British Museum, inv. GR 1842.7.28.712) of bronze, from southern Italy, dated to *c.* 320 BC. Originally connected to a back plate by a system of pins and hinges and ties at the shoulders, its *pteruges* are also missing. Funerary sculpture of the period shows three sets of *pteruges* protruding from the bottom of the corselet, rather than the two sets common in the previous century. These mid- to late-4th century BC corselets had separate shoulder guards, giving a double thickness of bronze at this point. The musculation on these is very much stylized and clearly designed to mimic an idealized male physique. This form of body armour was expensive. (Left – Wolfgang Sauber/ Wikimedia Commons/CC-BY-SA-4.0; Right – © Nic Fields)

[T]he nature of the site is like this: two deep defiles [*saltus duo alti*], narrow and wooded [*angusti silvosique*], are linked by an unbroken chain of mountains on either side. Between them lies an enclosed open area which is fairly extensive [*satis patens*], grassy and well watered [*herbidus aquosusque*], with the road running through the middle; [8] but before you come to it, you have to enter the first ravine and then either go back the same way you came in, or go out only by the other defile, which is narrower and more obstructed. (Liv. 9.2.7–8)

Unfortunately, this topographical narrative does not really match any of the possible upland routes in the locale of Caudium where the Samnite army was currently encamped. The location is obviously to be sought between Calatia and Caudium, the location of the Roman and the Samnite camps respectively, but none of the four likely candidates for the scene of the ambush have two narrow enough defiles to fit Livy's account of the Caudine Forks.

This brings us to the humanist antiquarian Flavio Biondo da Forlì (1392–1463). It was his major treatise *Italia illustrata*, 'Italy Illuminated', a rich and original historical, geographical and archaeological description of Italy, that made Biondo's reputation as the father of modern historiography and archaeology. A virtuoso scholar, his aim in this remarkable œuvre was to essentially connect present-day Italy (that is, of the mid-1400s) with its Roman and pre-Roman roots, thereby inviting the reader to survey a landscape and not only see the present populations, rivers, mountains and roads, but also to remember its long-distant past. Although Livy and Virgil are the authors most frequently cited in *Italia illustrata*, Biondo made good use of the chorographical scholarship of Strabo, the elder Pliny and Ptolemy. Anyway, having himself visited the area in question, in his learned opinion the valley of the little River Isclero, a short distance away, was the more likely location for the Caudine Forks (Biondo 1548, pp. 219–20, Sommella 1967, note 54). Most authorities still consider the narrow defiles to have been those that afforded access to the valley now called the Valle di Arienzo, by which passed the route from Capua to Beneventum (later the Via Appia).

OPPOSING PLANS

THE PATH TO WAR

It is reasonable to posit the idea that Rome's empire began with the Samnites. Though the urban-based state had increasingly extended its power and influence during the 5th century BC and the first half of the following century, conquering and integrating various Latin peoples and even the neighbouring Etruscan urban state of Veii, the extent of its territorial dominion was local and limited. Though the annexation of Veii and distribution of its land, the *ager Veientanus* (Liv. 5.30.8), has been seen as the first step on Rome's advance to an imperial power, it was really only with the Samnite wars that its reach began to extend beyond the immediate confines of Latium and southern Etruria, Roman arms grasping at the wealthy Italiote (viz. Greek) communities of Campania and the south. This is when we witness the real birth of empire in Rome.

The Samnites and the Samnite wars represent a key turning point for Rome, and the beginnings of an outward push. Additionally, although the Gauls of Gallia Cisalpina seem to have had the greatest impact on Rome's psyche during the 4th century BC, in large part of course because of the Gaulish sack of Rome, Rome's wars against the Samnites were to represent the greatest test of its armies.

The Gaulish onslaught at a crossing point of the Allia at its confluence with the Tiber near Crustumerium and mortally close to Rome, in 390 BC (according to Roman dating) or 387/386 BC (according to Greek dating), while not a complete surprise or sudden ambush, still seems to have caught the Romans somewhat unprepared. For it is recorded that their right wing fled in blind panic almost immediately in the face of the first Gaulish charge. Vividly portrayed by Livy (5.37.6–38), he has men drowning in the swirling waters of the Tiber, unable to swim or weakened by the weight of their war gear. However, while every subsequent meeting with the roving Gauls was seen as a major engagement (and the spectre of the Allia was evidently always lurking at the back of the collective Roman psyche, *metus Gallicus*, 'Gallic fear'), the Romans seem to have fared reasonably well against the Gauls during the rest of the century.[3]

---

3 The disaster was shocking, the day (18 July), *dies Alliensis*, 'the day of Allia', being forever remembered by the Romans as an *infaustus dies*, unlucky day (Liv. 6.1.11, Virg. *Aen.* 7.717, Tac. *Hist.* 2.91.1, Plut. *Cam.* 19.1), though for us moderns it is a battle long elbowed into literary limbo by its more spectacular sequel, the sack of Rome. See Liv. 4.34–55 and Polyb. 1.6.1 for the most detailed descriptions of the Gaulish sack.

The Samnites, by contrast, seem to have regularly tested the Roman army and, even after Rome's victory in the Third Samnite War of 298–290 BC, would remain a dormant but very real threat until the Social War of 90–88 BC, where the Samnites once again played a significant military role. When Pyrrhos of Epeiros challenged Rome in Italy, the Samnites rallied to his banner. Following the shattering defeat at Cannae, the Samnites, apart from the Pentri (Liv. 22.61.11), threw their support behind Hannibal. They were the prime movers during the Social War. Once the hostilities ended and Roman citizenship had been obtained, the Samnites took the field against Rome once more, on the occasion of the civil war that broke out on the return of Lucius Cornelius Sulla from his victories in the east (83 BC). Solidly on the side of that old warhorse and seven times consul Caius Marius (d. 86 BC), they were, together with the Marians, decisively defeated at the Battle of the Porta Collina (82 BC) just outside Rome, and exposed to the most brutal punishment by the victor Sulla. The dictators' vicious clearance of the vanquished was brutally effective, and never again did the Samnites rise up against Rome (Plut. *Sulla* 29–30.1, App. *B civ.* 1.93, Liv. *Per.* 88). Writing less than a century later, Strabo recounts this definitive, deliberate destruction of the Samnites:

> And to those who found fault with him for such excessive wrath he said he had realized from experience that not a Roman could ever live in peace so long as the Samnites [*Saunitai*] held together as a separate people. (Strab. 5.4.11)

LEFT: Montefortino helmet (Orvieto, Museo Archeologico Nazionale di Orvieto), from the Tomba del Guerriero near Porano, 4th century BC. With the pattern of three identical circles arranged to form a triangle, this example has cheek guards evidently modelled on the triple-disc cuirass. This helmet type is distinguished by its bulbous pointed shape and integral knob on the top, which serves as a crest (either a flowing horsehair plume or three upright feathers) holder. **RIGHT:** Montefortino helmet (Bologna, Museo Civico Archeologico, inv. 28233) from the Necropoli Benacci, Tomba 953, turn of the 3rd century BC. This pattern of helmet probably arrived in the Italian Peninsula with the Senonian Gauls at the end of the 5th century BC (Cascarino 2007, p. 104). (Left – Wolfgang Sauber/Wikimedia Commons/CC-BY-SA-4.0; Right – © Esther Carré)

There is something macabre about this desire in the victor to eradicate every trace of the vanquished. But then again, Sulla was a particularly chilling character.

Casus belli

World leaders are unusually hubristic and overconfident; for many, the fact that they have risen to elevated levels of power and privilege is evidence of the inherent wisdom. By all accounts, it looks as if we are plagued today with world leaders (many who have never worn uniform let alone heard the whistle of a hostile bullet) who are either tragically wrong-headed or openly reckless in leading their countries to war. When we turn to Rome, however, warfare formed an important part of elite identity going back to the early Iron Age, and Rome's aristocracy – although increasingly urbane and urban – retained a robust martial character throughout the Republican period.

In the 21st century, we know something about the tyranny of overseas wars started on false grounds. Yet this is no new thing. Equally, wars are easy to get into, but difficult to get out of. All soldiers and statesmen should heed the warning of Sun Tzu: 'there has never been a protracted war from which a country has benefited'.[4] The wars we have witnessed this century have

Bath building at the colony of Fregellae, which is a rare example of a non-religious public building from the 3rd century BC. For the year 328 BC, Livy has little to say regarding military and political events. He does, however, mention the establishment of the Latin colony of Fregellae, which was no minor event as it was the trigger for the outbreak of the Second Samnite War. Fregellae was located just east of the Liris (Liri), very close to its confluence with the Trerus (Sacco). This was recognized as Samnite territory, which had been won from the Volsci by force of arms – the upper course of the Liri was an early home to the Volsci. With this expansion into the Liris valley, conflict between Rome and the Samnites was in the offing. (Torquatus/ Wikimedia Commons/CC-BY-SA-4.0)

---

4   The first great work of military thought known to us, its concise aphorisms of enduring and timeless relevance and infinite application, is from China, the work of Sun Tzu. Dated between 400 BC and 320 BC (Griffith 1971 [1963], p. 11), the collection of essays called *The Art of War* is a treatise that is contemporaneous with the Caudine Forks.

LEFT: Triple-disc cuirass (Paestum, Museo Archeologico Nazionale di Paestum), Necropoli del Gaudo, Tomba 136, dated c. 420/400 BC. This burial belonged to a male aged 25 to 30 years of age. To date, nine examples of the triple-disc bi-valve cuirass have been found at Paestum, six dated to the period of 420–350 BC, and one to the late 4th century BC. Each consists of three symmetrical bronze discs front and back, thus forming two triangular plates, which are connected over the shoulders and across the sides by shoulder and side plates. These are attached by rings and hooks, while the shoulder plates are also hinged in the centre. The earliest examples have been recovered from the necropolis at Alfedena, Abruzzo, and are dated to the second half of the 5th century BC. RIGHT: Reconstruction of a triple-disc cuirass, Arverniales 2012, Gergovie, demonstrating the back plate and side plates of this bi-valve body armour. (Left – © Esther Carré; Right – Elliott Sadourny/Wikimedia Commons/CC-BY-SA-3.0)

largely resulted from a hawkish, regime-change-eager approach to foreign policy, failed leadership and miscalculations, mixed messages (invariably muscular in tenor), and the idealistic aspiration that somehow wars could be quickly won by easy victory. Wars always find people unprepared. Wars can be drawn out, both terrifying and tedious, hugely dangerous and utterly disorientating. Nothing is gained, nothing is learned, simply history repeated as tragic farce. A lot of these elements were conceivably played out in the confrontational relationship between Rome and the Samnites.

If we gloss over diagnosis of Polybios, a Greek observer with an acute eye and sharp intelligence, and stick to the letter of Livy's narrative and Cicero's rhetoric, then we have to believe that the Senate declared war almost exclusively in response to provocation or threat. So according to their own historical traditions, which were influenced by patriotic interests, the Romans refused to initiate a war of conquest without a just cause they could put before the people and the gods. There was, in other words, a conscious policy of defensive not aggressive imperialism. Apparently, therefore, to circumvent this conundrum, the Senate devised the devious political loophole of provoking the Samnites into initiating the war. It did this by belligerently planting Latin citizens in Samnite territory, calculating that its unwelcome presence there would sooner or later provoke the Samnites to fight. This was done at an out-of-the-way place on the River Liris called Fregellae, which was located at the frontier between Roman and Samnite supremacy, but just inside Samnium (Liv. 8.22.2).

Despite the loud noises of *bellum iustum*, a war permitted by law and by religion, in the Senate, the chosen site was a clever choice by its members. Situated on the Samnite bank of the Liris, Fregellae not only controlled a crossing of the river, but also the route through the valley of the River Trerus (the later Via Latina) and an undemanding way via a drove road over the Montes Auruncini, a mountain range that forms the lower flank of the valley of the Liris, to the Campanian Plain and the Tyrrhenian Sea. Furthermore, the colony blocked the north-western entrance to the middle Liris valley from Samnite raiding parties. In other words, Fregellae was perceived by the Romans as a nodal point astride a well-established network of communication routes commonly in the shape of drove roads (Lat. *calles*, It. *tratturi*) that criss-crossed the Apennines.

The Samnites reacted, as they were bound to do under the circumstances, by seeking a way to actively retaliate against Rome. This they did by intervening in Palaeopolis (later Neapolis, now Naples), a notional ally of Rome, by offering an alliance to the faction favourable to them. Despite the Greek colonial origin of Palaeopolis, the population probably already contained a substantial Oscan-speaking element (Strab. 5.4.7). During a meeting of its citizens, Palaeopolis opted to side with the Samnites and in doing so allowed them to garrison the city on their behalf (Dio. Hal. *Ant. Rom.* 15.5.5, 15.6.3). Now the Romans had to react, and they reacted promptly: without hesitation, a Roman army, commanded by the consul Quintus Publilius Philo, advanced to confront the Samnites, and besieged Palaeopolis. When the siege threatened to drag on beyond the term of Philo's consulship, the Senate introduced a new practice, one which would have a long-lasting effect on Rome's acquisition of empire: the extension of a magistrate's term of office in order to permit him to complete an ongoing mission (Liv. 8.22.23). This shrewd practice was termed prorogation, and the magistrate who was retained in office was termed a proconsul or propraetor, to distinguish him from the newly appointed consuls and the praetor (at this date there was only one). Unquestionably, Philo's mission necessitated persistence. Despite being hampered by internal instability, it was not easy to besiege Palaeopolis since its harbour allowed it to be supplied by sea. Even so, after a year of suffering the discomforts of war, the aristocrats of Palaeopolis delivered their city to the Romans, who promptly drove the Samnites from within. With the conquest – or liberation, depending on the point of view – of Palaeopolis, the Second Samnite War was on.

Livy, our source for this war, presents it as conflict between two rapidly expanding powers and a defining moment in the history of the Italian Peninsula, portraying a Samnite envoy as saying:

Panoramic view from Monte d'Oro, Parco Naturale dei Monti Aurunci, overlooking the Campanian Plain. Immediately below is the seaside resort of Scauri, which lies on the Golfo di Gaeta close to the mouth of the Garigliano, just visible in the middle distance. Mont d'Oro is part of the Monti Aurunci (Montes Auruncini), a mountain range of southern Lazio. It is part of the Antiapennini, a group running from the Apennine chain to the Tyrrhenian Sea, where it forms a promontory at Gaeta, ancient Caieta. (Gabriele Altimari/Wikimedia Commons/ CC-BY-SA-3.0)

'Our differences, Romans', he said, 'will be resolved neither by parleying between envoys nor by any man's arbitration, but by the plain of Campania where we must meet in battle, by the sword and the common fortune of war. Let us then pitch camp facing each other between Capua and Suessula and determine whether Samnites or Romans shall dominate Italy'. (Liv. 8.23.10)

Of course, this was written with a large helping of hindsight, and a great deal of simplification in order to make the confusing and chaotic events of this long and cruel conflict fit neatly into Livy's own vision of Roman history.

THE SAMNITE PLAN

Some battles are won before a single shot has been fired. Some battles indeed are forgone conclusions, the result seemingly written in the stars long before the campaign begins. And so it turned out, for the ambush and entrapment of the Romans at the Caudine Forks was of that nature. Ambushes have been around since the dawn of warfare and are still very much in vogue in modern combat. There is an Etruscan fresco in the Tomba dei Tori near Tarquinia which vividly portrays the young Trojan prince, the long-haired Troilus, being ambushed by his murderer, the swift-footed Achilles. Admittedly, this was a one-on-one event, but the same stratagem was employed on a much grander and more horrifying, genocidal scale by Saul against the Amalekites:

Saul went to the city of Amalek and set an ambush in the ravine … He took Agag king of the Amalekites alive, and all his people he totally destroyed with the sword. (1 Samuel 15:5, 8 NIV)

The Roman march to western Samnium

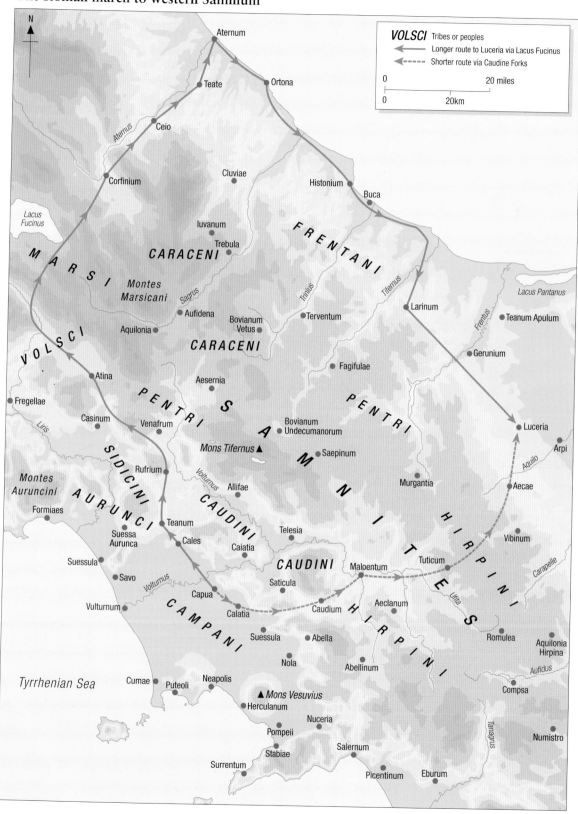

Saul had no trouble killing the Amalekite men and women, even their children and infants, cattle and sheep, camels and donkeys. The king was probably spared so as to serve as a trophy. Saul's ambush was a resounding success. Indeed, so long as there is war, there will be the art of the ambush.

With regards to their ambush at the Caudine Forks, the Samnites would not need to resort to biblical butchery. For they had several advantages: they had selected the target (the Romans), the time, the place and the nature of the attack. Vigilance on the part of the Romans could have helped negate some if not all of these advantages, particularly at critical points along the route – such as severely restricted terrain – when they should have been alert for ambushes.

If, as Clausewitz explained, 'war is thus an act of force to compel our enemy to do our will' (*Vom Krieg*, bk. 1, ch. 1, sec. 2, Howard and Paret p. 83), and if, as Sun Tzu realized, 'To capture the enemy's army is better than destroying it' (*The Art of War*), then if you make the enemy do what you want, you have won. In modern idiom this is known as 'reflexive control'. It goes beyond deception, becoming manipulation, much as a conjurer manipulates his audience. It sounds simple, but of course, nothing in war is ever simple. On the contrary, war is a most complex business, involving chance, luck, quick-thinking and exploiting any opportunity that arises. Even so, the Samnite commander Gavius Pontius believed he could subdue the Roman consular armies without engaging them. We will come back to that.

THE ROMAN PLAN

Livy (9.2.5) says the Romans were on their way to Apulia to relieve Luceria, having jointly decided to take the shortest route. Recent scholarship, however, has cast doubt over Rome's relationship with Luceria in 321 BC. E.T. Salmon, for instance, says 'Luceria was not even a friend, much less a beleaguered ally, of Rome at this time' (2010 [1967], p. 224, note 6). Whatever their intentions, the two consuls advanced into the Caudine Forks, two wooded defiles with a grassy vale, wider but still surrounded by craggy heights, between them. The Samnite League generalissimo, obviously well informed about the Romans and their intentions, concealed his men and blocked the further defile with a defended barricade of felled trees and boulders. The consuls continued on their way, quite unaware that they were walking straight into a trap. Of course, the historian's *ex post facto* knowledge should not necessarily prejudice him or her against the consuls' decision. Actually, there is an argument to be made that this may have been an attempt to force a decisive success by knocking the Oscan Caudini out of the war. A good idea, if they had got away with it.

THE CAMPAIGN

As far as we can fathom, the Second Samnite War was not in fact a single, continuous event, but one that fell into three distinct phases: (1) 326–321 BC, characterized by Roman yearly campaigns in or near Samnium, marked by a number of Roman victories – the *Fasti Triumphales* record triumphs over the Samnites in 325 BC and twice in 322 BC with the Samnites then offering peace, which was roundly rejected – but concluding with the humiliation at the Caudine Forks; (2) 321–317 BC, known as the Caudine Peace, a period of four years during which the Romans and the Samnites did not fight against one another; and (3) 316–304 BC, during which the war was resumed and, after an initial Samnite victory at Lautulae in 315 BC, the Romans eventually prevailed after a protracted struggle which involved the Etruscans and Umbri too.

Varco della Capriola, Parco Nazionale d'Abruzzo, Lazio e Molise. The Apennine landscape is one completely given over to massifs, with its lunatic jumble of pointed peaks, bare rock piles, sheer-sided ravines and knife-edge ridges. Even in the height of summer this is harsh and difficult land to negotiate. (Francesco Cosentino/ Wikimedia Commons/ CC-BY-SA-4.0)

THE ROAD TO HUMILIATION

Though Livy's narrative of the conflict tends to shoehorn this into a tidier narrative of coherent campaigns and pitched battles, a chaotic series of inconclusive skirmishes and frontier raids was more likely the order of the day for the first five years of the war. These speedy strikes were undoubtedly carried out by comparatively small bodies of men, with the yearly Roman consuls acting independently of each other. In order to end this five-year impasse, it appears the Senate attempted to adopt a more pugnacious stance against the Samnites, strong in battle, by suggesting the pooling of the forces of both consuls and advancing into the territory of the Caudini, the most westerly and therefore the most exposed of the Samnite polities.

It therefore needs to be observed that a large majority of the yearly military operations were limited to raids with sporadic pitched battles in the countryside. The storming of key urban communities was extremely rare; and sieges even more so. The taking of subsidiary or minor urban centres was, on the other hand, more common. Unless one of these events occurred, it was very unusual for Roman soldiers to enter walls, and even less to be allowed to loot, a major conurbation. This was the treatment that was commonly meted out to farmsteads, hamlets and villages. After all, looting was an essential and ubiquitous component of warfare, and had been one since long before the Second Samnite War. The earlier fate of Veii,

for instance, was rather exceptional in this regard, and during the course of this particular war very few other rich Italian urban-based communities were besieged, stormed or sacked, let alone their population lumped with that of Rome. As we have seen in the case of Veii, the siege and sack of the Samnite stronghold of Saticula in 315 BC would be a distant outlier.

The new Roman consuls of 321 BC were ambitious, but militarily inexperienced, Titus Veturius Calvinus and Spurius Postumius Albinus.[5] Agreeing to pool their two consular armies, they were determined to inflict, once and for all, a crippling blow on the Samnites. As for the size of this combined force, the numbers given by our extant sources have been grossly exaggerated: 40,000 (Dio. Hal. *Ant. Rom.* 16.3) or 50,000 (App. *Sam.* 4.2). There are no figures for the Samnite army.

That year, the Samnite League had elected a generalissimo of exceptional talent, Gavius Pontius, son of Herennius Pontius, a man who was clearly thinking bigger than his two Roman opponents. In the words of Livy, the Samnite generalissimo was *primum ipsum bellatorem ducemque*, 'unrivalled in military ability and leadership' (9.1.2). After an earlier olive branch was rebuked by Rome, Gavius Pontius assembled his army and took to the field, determined to force a peace where one could not be negotiated.

From his camp outside Caudium, Gavius Pontius despatched ten of his warriors disguised as shepherds into Roman territory on a mission to spread false rumours and misleading information and so put the enemy off guard. The deceit in the form of blatant lies worked a treat. When questioned by foraging parties, the Samnite spies all informed

Largo di Telese, Telese Terme, Campania. Telese Terme was an ancient settlement of the Oscan Caudini, known as T(h)elesia, and the likely birthplace of Gavius Pontius – some writers of late antiquity actually give him the *cognomen* Telesinus (e.g. Eutr. 10.17.2), which was certainly the native settlement of later Pontii (*ILS* 6510), including Pontius Telesinus, the Samnite commander during the Social War (91–88 BC) and subsequently during Sulla's second civil war (83–81 BC), who claimed descent from the present hero. Situated on the right bank of the Calor (Calore) at its junction with the Volturnus (Volturno), and a little north of the great bulk of Taburno Camposauro, Telesia served as an important nodal point. (silvio sicignano/ Wikimedia Commons/ CC-BY-SA-2.0)

5   They had been consuls together previously, in 334 BC, when they oversaw the colonization of Cales in Campania (Liv. 8.16.12).

The rebuilt Abbey of Monte Cassino, the first house of the Benedictine Order (AD 524), seen from the Roma–Napoli Highway. The valley of the Liri was the chosen site for the much later Gustav Line, a truly formidable example of German military engineering that barred the Allies from the gateway to Rome. Supplementing nature with steel and concrete, mines and wire, this defensive line ran along the northern rim of the Liri valley, hemmed in as it was by mountains, through Monte Cassino (elev. 520m) and into the massif of Cairo, of which the highest peak is Monte Cairo (elev. 1,669m) to the north of the monastery. In our period of study Cassino was known as Casinum, a mountain stronghold that controlled one of the principal access points into Samnium. (ModriDirkac/Wikimedia Commons/CC0 1.0)

the Romans that the Samnite League army was far away besieging the border settlement of Luceria (Lucera), seemingly a recent Roman ally and certainly a later colony of theirs in Apulia. The Romans, as planned, mobilized under the consuls and began preparations to come to the aid of their Lucerian allies.

If Livy is correct with regards to the status of this Apulian settlement as being *bonis ac fidelibus sociis*, 'good and loyal allies' (9.2.5), then it is reasonable to believe that, for reasons of reputation and reliability, the Senate would want to support the Lucerians militarily. There were two routes to Luceria from the current Roman camp near Calatia, just to the east of Capua and on the fringes of Samnite and Campanian territories. The first went via the Lacus Fucinus (drained in 1878) in Abruzzo and skirted the Adriatic coast, 'and though open and unobstructed, was long almost in portion to its safety' (Liv. 9.2.6). The second was much shorter, but passed through the Caudine Forks, a key entry point into western Samnium. They consisted of an open grassy and well-watered upland valley surrounded by densely wooded slopes and overhangs. The road (later the Via Appia) ran

through the centre and was bookended by two deep defiles, narrow and wooded, through the surrounding mountains (ibid. 9.2.7–8) – an unpeopled rawness, just the tall trees and the ragged rocks. It was along the latter that the two consuls decided to march their combined consular armies, thereby opting to take the shortest route in the shortest time. The consuls themselves had abundant confidence – too much, we suspect. The stage was being set for a disaster.

The Romans advanced headlong into a Samnite trap. They found the eastern exit point from the Caudine Forks closed by a barricade of boulders and felled trees with limbs sharpened, making a sort of abattis, which was manned by the Samnites. The marching Romans, on reaching the barricade, made an attempt to carry it, failed and retraced their steps in haste, only to discover that the defile by which they had entered was also blocked with its own defended barricade. Clearly, like its eastern counterpart, the Samnite field fortification was a formidable challenge. To make matters worse, Samnite warriors soon appeared on the beetling heights overlooking their entrapped foes.

Using an intimate knowledge of the local terrain, what Gavius Pontius had done in effect was to set a deliberate ambush. This, as we shall discuss in due course, is based upon extensive knowledge of the enemy, ground and the enemy's use of that ground; and the ambush site and the specific target to be ambushed are known. At Caudine Forks, this allowed Gavius Pontius to maximize exploitation during the execution of the ambush.

The Romans were excellent fighters down on the flat lands or out in the open countryside, but they were poorly prepared for the unfamiliar and chaotically mountainous backbone of central Italy. The upland valley had become a death trap. In the words of Livy:

> [A] stupor came over the minds of all, and a strange kind of numbness over their bodies; and looking at one another – for every man supposed his neighbour more capable of thinking and planning than himself – stood for a long time motionless and silent. (Liv. 9.2.10–11)

Panoramic view of the Valle Caudina, Campania, viewed from Monte Paraturo (elev. 927m), part of the Monti del Partenio massif. To the left is Monte Tairano (elev. 768m), below which is the Stretta di Arpaia. In the centre distance sits Monte Taburno, part of Taburno Camposauro, the massif that rises above the Valle Caudina to the north. The SS7 Appia road, which follows the original Via Appia, is visible on the right traversing the town of Arpaia and heading north-east towards Benevento (which the Romans called Beneventum and the Samnites Malventum – Osc. *Maloenton*, Gk. *Maloventum*). This settlement was some 15km from Caudium, the principal urban settlement of the Caudini. As the SS7 Appia exits the valley at its eastern end, it passes through a narrow defile below Monte Taburno known as the Passo di Sferracavallo. The western defile out of the Valle di Arienzo can be seen in the left-hand corner. (Decan/Wikimedia Commons/CC-BY-SA-4.0)

THE ROMAN COLUMN OF MARCH ENTERS THE WESTERN DEFILE (PP. 52–53)

Livy describes the Caudine Forks, *Furculae Caudinae*, as formed by two narrow wooded defiles, between which lay an upland valley, verdant and well-watered, but entirely enclosed by the surrounding mountains. Through this valley passed the route from Capua in Campania to Beneventum in Samnium.

In this plate we see the Roman consular armies (**1**), having marched that morning from their last camp near Calatia, now heading for Caudium, strung out in column of march. The head of the column is just entering the valley unopposed through the western defile. All is seemingly serene; there is no sign of the Samnites. Pack animals can be seen towards the rear of the column (**2**).

However, two Samnite warriors are monitoring the passage of the Roman marching column carefully. Both wear the distinctive Oscan broad belt (**3**). The standing warrior wears triple-disc cuirass body armour (**4**), while his companion to the left sports a simpler style of body protection (**5**). He has removed his Italo-Attic helmet, and it lies on the ground (**6**). They are armed with *hastae* (thrusting spears, **7**) and *xiphoi* (double-edged, straight shortswords) housed in scabbards suspended from baldrics (**8**).

Terrain is not just the field where the battle is fought – it is very much a part of the battle itself. A commander who makes the terrain work in a positive manner against the enemy can restrict the mobility of his army, which can even put it in a fatal position.

In his battle descriptions, Livy was more interested in psychological insight than technical factors. This being said, we can be prepared to forgive him for, or at least overlook, his evident literary attempt to enliven an otherwise dry battle account; for it is easy to visualize the bewilderment of the Roman rank and file upon the realization of their perilous predicament. Closely hemmed in all round and faced with possible death or captivity, the soldiers of Rome were caught in a very difficult situation, and their terror and isolation must have been palpable. The skilfully laid ambush at Caudine Forks was an example of near-perfect military planning and execution.

Trapping the Romans allowed the Samnites to gain and maintain the initiative, as the enemy was forced to react to their actions. It also eventually undermined the Romans' will to resist when they were at their weakest. Though the silence of Livy gives the clear impression there was no battle as such, there was evidently some fighting at the barricades, at least that is what Cicero implies:

> *a quo Caudino proelio Sp. Postumius, T. Veturius consules superati sunt …*
> at the Caudine Forks routed the two consuls, Spurius Postumius and Titus Veturius … (Cic. *Sen.* 12.41, cf. P.Oxy. I 12 ad an. 320/319 BC)

After vain attempts to cut their way out of one or both of the defiles – we shall never know for sure – the entrapped consular armies attempted to fortify their position somewhere in the valley, undoubtedly near a reliable water source. But it was fruitless. Everybody knew, be it friend or foe, that all the Samnites had to do was to wait for Roman supplies to run out and let hunger become the main weapon to defeat their foe. So, as the Romans worked, the Samnites waited.

Realism in due course was to break out as nervousness, and then panic stepped in. As fear began to lay its cold dead hand upon them, the consuls surrendered ostensibly to avoid starvation. In the stoic, lean light of predawn, all was lost, including hope and honour.

LEFT: Detail of the Situla della Certosa (Bologna, Museo Civico Archeologico, inv. 124), Necropoli della Certosa, Tomba 68, dated *c.* 600/550 BC. *Situlae* were bucket-shaped vessels of sheet copper alloy, some plain, others highly decorated like that from Certosa. This is the top frieze of *repoussé* (raised decoration hammered through the reverse side), which depicts a military parade of warriors, four equipped with the *clipeus* and three with the Italic body shield, or *scutum*. **RIGHT:** Schematic showing the two decorative zones of the Arnoaldi Situla, Necropoli Arnoaldi, Tomba 104, dated 500/450 BC. Two friezes of *repoussé* depict a military parade of chariots and warriors, all the latter bar one carrying the *scutum*. (Left – Sailko/Wikimedia Commons/CC-BY-SA-3.0; Right – © Esther Carré)

NO MIDDLE WAY

On 27 April 1799, Aleksandr Vasilevitch Suvorov won the Battle of Cassano d'Adda and then entered Milan. Here was a warrior who had

THE ROMANS ATTEMPT TO BREAK OUT THROUGH THE EASTERN DEFILE (PP. 56–57)

Having penetrated what turned out to be an ambush site, the Romans (**1**) discovered the exit through the second defile at the eastern end of the valley had been barricaded by the Samnites. As a military maxim spells out, 'an obstacle not covered by fire is little more than a nuisance to the enemy's movement': in other words, it is not an obstacle. This is the fundamental rule: any obstacle can be surmounted given time, energy and no distractions. At this stage, despite the apparent hopelessness of their situation, the Romans would have attempted to break through the entrapment. However, at this end of the valley the Samnites (**2**) soon revealed themselves and manned their barricade.

In this plate we witness the Romans mounting an assault in a brave attempt (in vain, as it would turn out) to carry the obstacle across their path. The Samnite defenders are holding the Roman onslaught from behind their barricade, made of boulders, felled trees, earth and an abatis of sharpened tree branches.

The Roman officer to the left (**3**) is a wealthier citizen, equipped with the panoply of the Greek hoplite, with helmet and muscled cuirass of bronze, and the *clipeus* (double-grip bowl-shaped shield). His Italo-Corinthian helmet has a transverse crest and upright feathers. His sword is the *kopis*, a type which had a single-edged recurved blade that pitched towards its point.

The figure to the right (**4**) is a less well-off Roman citizen, wearing a simple pectoral plate secured into place by means of a harness in the form of leather cross straps. He carries the oval *scutum* body shield, Italic in origin, and wears a Montefortino helmet with cheek pieces. The less well-off citizens might be armed only with a *hasta*, the long thrusting spear.

Full-scale reconstruction of an Italic body shield, Los Villares, Caudete de las Fuentes, Valencia. Italic in origin, the *scutum* was very much like the θυρεός/*thureós* ('door-like') common to peltasts of later Hellenistic armies. It had only a single, horizontal handgrip in the centre, protected by a large metal boss plate. This allowed it to be moved about freely, and the boss plate could be used offensively, too, by punching the enemy. The shield board is thicker in the centre and flexible at the edges, making it very resilient to blows, and the top and bottom edges may have been reinforced with bronze or iron edging to prevent splitting. Nailed to the front and running vertically from top to bottom is a wooden spine. Archaeological evidence reveals that the *scutum* was in general use among the various Italic peoples well before the Romans and Samnites ever came to blows. (Dorieo/Wikimedia Commons/ CC-BY-SA-3.0)

several wars under his belt, and before engaging with the French at Cassano, he explained to his soldiers how thorough he expected them to be: 'Pursue the last man to the Adda and throw the remains into the river'. Plainly, in war one must be ready to risk all to gain all; there was no finding the middle ground. It has to be said, however, that it is not certain the Samnite generalissimo Gavius Pontius fully understood this eternal truth. For all his outstanding generalship, to say that Gavius Pontius had no idea what to do so as to take advantage of his spectacular success at the Caudine Forks is an understatement. He decided to dash off a communiqué to his father Herennius Pontius. The wise old man, who had debated with the philosophers Plato and Archytas at Taras, stated his opinion bluntly in a return memorandum. The Romans should be allowed to depart at once, uninjured and unmolested. The younger Pontius and his war council dismissed the suggestion. Would it not negate their brilliant victory? A second communiqué was sent to Herennius, and a very different answer came back in reply. Herennius' terrible commandment was that all the Romans, to the very last man, should be put to the sword. Was the old man senile?

Clearly he was, thought Gavius Pontius and his war council, having given such contradictory answers to the same question. The elder Pontius was invited to the camp to explain himself. At the convening of the council on his arrival, Herennius explained his reasoning to the gathered Samnite officers:

> If, he said, they adopted his first proposal – which he held to be best – they would establish lasting peace and friendship with a very powerful people by conferring an enormous benefit upon them; by adopting the other plan they would postpone the war for many generations, in which time the Roman state, having lost two armies, would not easily regain its strength; there was no third plan. (Liv. 9.3.10)

So, in Herennius' considered opinion, there was no middle way, for that would be utter folly and leave Rome smarting for revenge without weakening it. And Rome was just stubborn enough to do that. As oppose to aiming for the Aristotelian belief of moderation among unequals, Herennius' paradigm of ethics stipulated extreme response to extremes. That, sadly, was not what Gavius Pontius thought. In his mind, the prisoners should be forced to shamefully scuttle back to Rome. After all, it was the victory deserved by the Samnites, and the defeat deserved by the Romans. Herennius was not to be shaken from his cold logic: 'whatever shame you brand them with in their present necessity, the wound will ever rankle in their bosoms, nor will it suffer them to rest until they have exacted many times as heavy a penalty of you' (Liv. 9.3.13). This was, of course, a remarkably prescient analysis.

Valle di Arienzo viewed from the Collina del Castello d'Arienzo (elev. 623m), the castle dismantled by Roger II of Sicily in 1135. The peak on the left is Monte Pianitella (elev. 626m); while in the right distance is the narrower eastern defile (near Arpaia) leading out of the upland valley. The Valle di Arienzo is traditionally recognized as the location of the Caudine Forks. However, neither defile leading to it is as narrow and steep as Livy suggests. The western one, nearest to the town of Arienzo (seen below centre), is over a kilometre wide, which makes it unlikely that the Samnites had enough time to block it effectively in the brief time the Romans would have taken to cross the valley to the eastern defile and return, the distance being only 4.5km. Still, the *campus* itself is, as Livy (9.2.7) says, *satis patens* and *herbidus*, even if not exactly *aquosus*. (Antonio De Capua/Wikimedia Commons/ CC-BY-SA-4.0)

Ignoring his father's Nestor-like sapience, Gavius Pontius would make the Romans pass under the yoke. In his scrutiny of all this, Niccolò Machiavelli was to write the following:

> At all costs should the middle be avoided; for it is hurtful, as it was to the Samnites when they caught the Romans in the Caudine Forks and were unwilling to follow the advice of the old man who told them either to treat the Romans as honourable men and to set them free, or to kill the lot. For they took the middle course, disarmed them, marched them under the yoke and then set them free, burning with shame and indignation. With the result that, later on, they learned to their cost that the old man's advice was sound and their own decision harmful … (Machiavelli *Discorsi* 2.23)

In all probability deeply saddened, the old man left his son to relish in his short-lived triumph. Nevertheless, Gavius Pontius would forever wear the glamour of that magnificent victory at the Caudine Forks. Still, to follow up on the scrutiny of Machiavelli:

> This victory, which Pontius gained by fraud, would have resounded greatly to his credit had he followed his father's advice, which was that he should either let the Romans go scot-free or should slaughter them all, and that he should not take the middle course which 'neither makes you friends, nor removes your enemies' [quoted from Liv. 9.3.12]; and this middle course has always been harmful in the affairs of state. (Machiavelli *Discorsi* 3.40)

Interestingly enough, the story of a father's advice to his son, and how his son went against every piece of it, would in a later period become a common form of European fable.

Montesarchio, Campania, which is identified as ancient Caudium, a town on the western side of the Apennines in the Valle Caudina. In the centre is the cylindrical Torre di Montesarchio and to the right the Castello di Montesarchio, built primarily during the Aragonese rule of the Kingdom of Naples. Beyond are the rocky southern slopes of Taburno Camposauro, its highest peaks being Monte Taburno (elev. 1,393m) in the south (seen here) and Monte Camposauro (elev. 1,390m) in the north. The Romans knew the massif by the name *Taburnus*, and it is mentioned twice by Virgil (*Aen.* 12.715, *G.* 2.38). Montesarchio is the site of a necropolis, which has yielded around 3,000 burials stretching from the 8th century BC to the Roman period. When they took Caudium, the Romans changed the name to *Mons Arcis*, hence Montesarchio. (Salvatore Di Maro/Wikimedia Commons/CC-BY-SA-3.0)

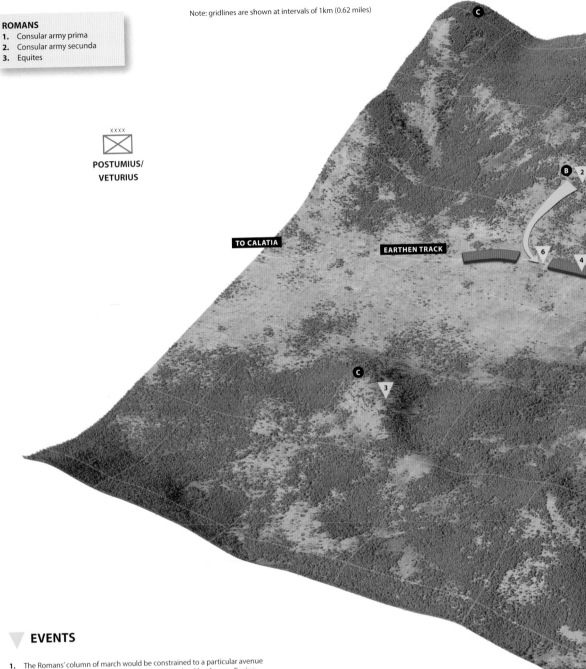

Note: gridlines are shown at intervals of 1km (0.62 miles)

ROMANS
1. Consular army prima
2. Consular army secunda
3. Equites

POSTUMIUS/
VETURIUS

TO CALATIA

EARTHEN TRACK

EVENTS

1. The Romans' column of march would be constrained to a particular avenue of approach due to the restrictions imposed by the upland landscape. Gavius Pontius predicted this and so made the most of what nature had presented. He thus establishes a blocking force at the eastern defile, which defends a readymade barricade of boulders, felled timber, earth and other material locally available.

2. In the heights above the western defile, Gavius Pontius conceals a second blocking force in preparation to block entrance into the Caudine Forks once the Romans have entered the valley and are well within the ambush site.

3. Additionally, the higher elevations above the western defile provide excellent observation points. Lookouts thus positioned overlooking the route from Calatia. At the same time, small bands of warriors are established in concealed positions at various points along the slopes overlooking the valley below.

4. In the meantime, the Romans are marching to Caudium, strung out along the route from Calatia; they advance eastwards without reconnaissance.

5. Once the two consuls and their armies have marched through the western defile and are now a good way into the valley, Gavius Pontius springs his trap.

6. The western blocking force comes out of hiding and commences to bar the western defile with boulders, felled trees, earth and all manner of obstructions that had already been assembled but well hidden beforehand. At the same time, the small bands appear on the slopes above the valley; the consuls now understand the trap into which they have been led.

7. At this point, Gavius Pontius holds the Roman armies at his mercy, and their destruction, if so wishes it, would be only a matter of time. Nonetheless, the Romans recover their wits and attempt to break out of the trap through the barricade blocking the eastern defile.

8. The Samnites beat back the Roman assault.

9. The Romans, bruised and battered, retreat towards the centre of the valley and attempt to fortify their position.

CAUDINE FORKS: AMBUSH SET AND SPRUNG

Livy (9.2) describes the location of the Caudine Forks ambush as follows: 'there are two passes, deep, narrow, with wooded hills on each side, and a continuous chain of mountains extends from one to the other. Between them lies a watered grassy plain through the middle of which the road goes. Before you reach the plain you have to pass through the first defile and either return by the same path by which you entered or, if you go on, you must make your way out by a still narrower and more difficult pass at the other end.' Shown here are the events of the entrapment of the Romans by Samnite forces along the grassy plain.

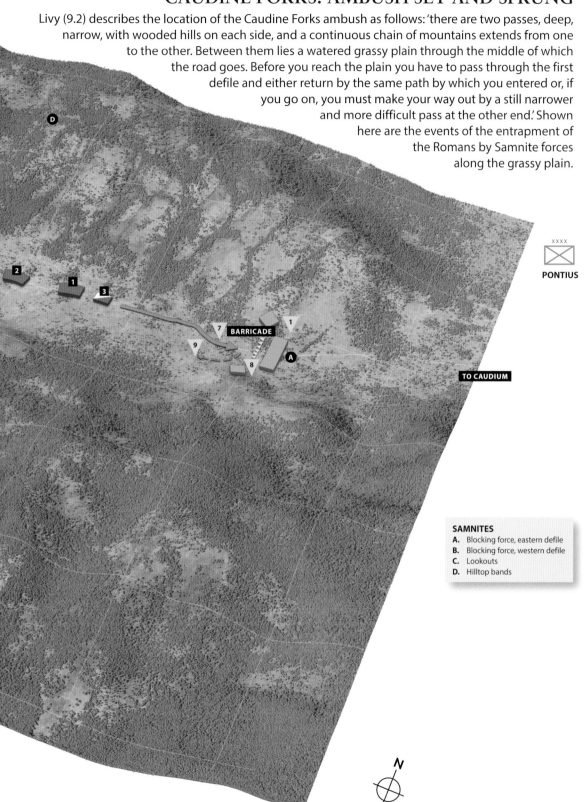

PONTIUS

BARRICADE

TO CAUDIUM

SAMNITES
A. Blocking force, eastern defile
B. Blocking force, western defile
C. Lookouts
D. Hilltop bands

N

UNCONDITIONAL SURRENDER

For the Samnites, the ostensible object was to create a *foedus* (treaty) with Rome that allowed them to live in peace. The main object – *pax*, peace – is stated by Livy at the beginning of book IX, with reference to the failed Samnite delegation: *legati qui ad dedendas res missi erant pace infecta redierunt*, 'the envoys who had been sent with the terms of surrender returned from their fruitless mission' (Liv. 9.1.3). It is repeated as one of Pontius' terms in the *sponsio: alias condiciones pacis aequas victis ac victoribus fore*, 'the other conditions would be fair to both victors and vanquished' (Liv. 9.4.3). With the entrapped consular armies in their power, the Samnites announced the terms on which they were willing to make this peace with Rome. These terms, three in number, are essentially conditions, namely, that: first, Rome withdraw from Samnium (Liv. 9.4.4); second, Rome remove its colonies, *coloniae abducerentur*, from Samnite territory (op. cit.); and third, that each side retain its own laws, *suis inde legibus* (op. cit.). Finally, Gavius Pontius demanded that the Romans accept all three conditions. If they did not, the envoys were not to return (Liv. 9.4.5), which obviously left no room for negotiation: it was a 'take it or leave it' deal that was especially hard for the Romans to accept.

Worse was to come. For there were, in addition, two ancillary Samnite conditions: first, the unconditional surrender of the consular armies, which would leave disarmed according to the traditional rules of war, under the yoke, *inermes cum singulis vestimentis sub iugum missurum*, 'unarmed under the yoke retaining one garment each' (Liv. 9.4.3), and; second, as a guarantee that the Romans ratify the proposed treaty, 600 *equites* were to be held under guard. The hostages were to be returned, if the treaty was ratified, but might be executed if it was not (Liv. 9.5.5).

THE FINAL ACT: THE YOKE OF SPEARS

We now turn back to the Roman camp, and to the events following the terms of surrender. In an admission of utter defeat, the Roman soldiers, valued citizens of Rome to a man, were disarmed and then required to quit the field by passing under the yoke, bending low to the ground, and as they did so *prope seminudi*, 'almost half-naked', in a humiliating ritual 'gloomier than death'; some committed suicide rather than endure it (Liv. 9.6.1–2, cf. Dio 5.7.17). The very pan-Italic symbol of ignominious defeat, the yoke was a frame made from two spears stuck in the ground with a third one lashed across horizontally at a height that compelled the semi-naked Roman soldiers to crouch down underneath: having done so, the last shreds of self-esteem and security were stripped from the individual. The yoke itself was symbolic of submission and servility of the vanquished to the supremacy and superiority of the victors.

We are told the Romans emerged from the Caudine Forks shuffling in silence and abject despair. Meanwhile, in Rome news of the unconditional surrender at the Caudine Forks, no doubt magnified by rumour and hearsay, could only have alarmed the citizens of the capital. Appian states that in Rome, 'the women mourned for those who had been saved in this ignominious way, as for the dead', and that all marriages for those who had been saved were suspended for a year (*Sam.* 4.7, cf. Liv. 9.9.7). In his concluding remarks on the Roman disaster at the Caudine Forks, Livy has this to say:

Valle Caudina, Campania, seen from Monte Taburno. The upland valley runs roughly north–south below Montesarchio, ancient Caudium, and in the centre left is the Castello di Montesarchio, while beyond rises the Monti del Partenio massif. The Valle Caudina is seen by some scholars as the location for the Caudine Forks. Being delimited by Monte Taburno in the north and Monti del Partenio in the south means the valley is well enclosed by mountain heights, a point in favour of those who position the Samnite ambush here. Moreover, it has two narrow access defiles: one leading out of the Valle di Arienzo at its western end (the Stretta di Arpaia, seen right distance), and the Passo di Sferracavallo at its eastern end, through which the SS7 Appia passes en route to Benevento. However, there is one crucial objection to this being the actual location of the ambush site: in 321 BC, the Valle Caudina was dominated by the settlement of Caudium. (Decan/Wikimedia Commons/ CC-BY-SA-4.0)

THE TWO CONSULS NEGOTIATE WITH THE SAMNITE GENERALISSIMO (PP. 66–67)

Gavius Pontius (**1**), the Samnite generalissimo, is depicted in a short linen tunic and an Oscan broad bronze belt (**2**). This is a leather belt, some 9cm in breadth and covered with bronze sheeting, fastened with two elaborate hooks and beautifully embossed. Accentuating the waist and drawing attention to the groin area, it is the very symbol of the wearer's manhood. Prominent, however, is his splendid gilded bronze body armour (**3**), the triple-disc cuirass peculiar to an Oscan warrior. This consists of three symmetrical bronze discs placed on the chest and the back. Our fine example is based upon that found in a chamber tomb at Ksour Essef, Tunisia, which has the lower disc replaced with a bust of a goddess adorned with a triple-crested helmet. She is probably the Oscan equivalent of Athena Promachos, 'Athena who fights in the front line', a very appropriate divine patron for the shrewd Gavius Pontius.

The Roman political system consisted of a series of annually elected magistrates, with two consuls acting as the chief executive magistrates of the state, as well as its supreme military commanders in the field. The two consuls for the year 321 BC, Titus Veturius Calvinus (**4**) and Spurius Postumius Albinus (**5**), like their adversary, are both decked out in their finest panoply. This consists of an Italo-Corinthian helmet (**6**), a peculiar and perverted development of the closed Greek Corinthian helmet once commonly worn by hoplites. These helmets, which are silvered, are adorned with a horsehair crest. Their body armour consists of Etruscan muscle-corselets (**7**), likewise silvered, complete with shoulder guards and *pteruges*. Beneath this they wear fine linen tunics, which have been bleached white.

Though the Samnite and the two Romans in all probability understand one another's language, Oscan and Latin respectively, so as not to misunderstand the finer points of their discussions they are accompanied by interpreters (**8** and **9**) speaking in Attic Greek, the lingua franca of diplomacy. Gavius Pontius has also brought with him his two Molossian hounds (**10**), for added protection.

The Samnites now perceived that instead of their domineering peace, they were confronted with the renewal of a most bitter war, and not only imagined but almost saw all the consequences which afterwards proceeded from it. (Liv. 9.12.1)

It was to be the last time that Rome accepted peace as the clear loser in a conflict.

The moral vision was part and parcel of the annalistic tradition, and this is evident in the way Livy presents the Caudine Forks, since his version clearly unfolds as a cautionary tale. Even if only a parable, his account serves as a powerful illustration that the middle way is not always the best. For the unfavourable treaty that followed this serious and humiliating reverse for Rome, an ignominious disaster to rank alongside the Allia debacle, meant instead the Samnites inherited a war that never really ended, but rather spilled out into cascades of further violence.

THE FALLOUT

What happened after the Caudine Forks is a matter of some conjecture. As already mentioned, Livy says that the truce between the Romans and the Samnites was not a *foedus*, treaty, but a *sponsio*, a solemn oath to which the oath-takers acted as guarantors. Such agreements were provisional suspensions of hostilities made by the commanders on the ground, and had to be ratified by the authorities back home if they were to become binding. The Senate had a different attitude. The senators, appalled by the humiliation, tore up the agreement and wanted to hand over the consuls, who had acted as sponsors, to the Samnites to face their wrath; the senators

Arpaia, Campania, traditionally believed to be the site of the Romans passing under the yoke following the entrapment of the two consular armies and their subsequent surrender at the Caudine Forks, at sunset. Left is Monte Paraturo, right is Monte Tairano, and between the two is the eastern defile, the Stretta di Arpaia, leading out of the Valle di Arienzo. In the foreground sits the town of Arpaia. Forchia, a town just a couple of kilometres or so from Arpaia, also lays claim to being the site of this infamous episode. The dispute between the two communes is relatively recent. In 1947, the prefect of Arpaia wrote an inscription, which he then had engraved on the façade of the town hall, advertising the claim. Forchia soon retaliated by pointing out the fact that the name of the town sounds like *Forche*, and there is even an old monastery nearby named *Santa Maria del Giogo*, Saint Mary of the Yoke. (Decan/Wikimedia Commons/ CC-BY-SA-4.0)

THE ROMANS SURRENDER THEIR ARMS AND ARMOUR (PP. 70–71)

The Samnite tunic (1) was a short garment of wool or linen with short sleeves and a rounded neckline, and either a straight, rounded or pointed hemline. Bands of decorated material were applied to the shoulders, sleeves, hem and chest, and the examples depicted in this artwork reconstruction are based on the funerary paintings from Paestum and south Italian red-figure vases, the *tunicae versicolores* of Livy (9.40.3). By contrast, the Roman soldiers are clothed in the cheapest undyed woollen cloth; consequently, we see them depicted wearing tunics of a natural off-white colour.

Here we see a procession of dispirited Roman soldiers (2), having tossed down their arms and armour, submitting themselves to the disgrace of passing under the yoke (3). They pass between two throngs of Samnite warriors (4), who look on, jeering at and taunting the humiliated Romans with understandable satisfaction. Some have erected trophies of Roman weapons and armour, hoisted on the tops of their spears (5).

had decided that Spurius Postumius and Titus Veturius had exceeded their authority in consenting terms to Gavius Pontius. The Senate then mustered an army the following year, which went on the warpath to avenge the disgrace, inflicting defeats on the Samnites, freeing Roman prisoners of war, and forcing 7,000 captured Samnites, including Gavius Pontius himself, under the yoke (Liv. 9.15.7–8).

Naturally, many modern commentators believe that these post-Caudine Forks events have been fabricated so as to gloss over the humiliation, and that the peace, concluded by means of a *foedus* rather than a *sponsio*, held good until 316 BC. Cicero (*Inv. rhet.* 2.91) evidently believed that a *foedus* was signed between the two warring parties. Others, on the other hand, point out that this version of the annalistic narrative represents a rather bizarre exercise in face-saving, as it depicts the Romans as oath-breakers – not a thing to be done lightly, since oath-making was a religious ritual – and that a triumph recorded in the *Fasti Triumphales* for 319/318 BC for victories in Samnium and Apulia provides some corroborative evidence for Roman campaigns in southern Italy, as does Diodorus Siculus (19.10.1–2) in Apulia for the same campaigning season. Ultimately, we have no way of recovering what in actual fact happened immediately post-Caudine Forks.

What we do know is that the phoney peace, or *pax Caudina*, to employ the term repeatedly used by Livy (9.1.1, 9.7.4, 9.8.1, 9.12.3), would be broken when Rome undeniably resumed the struggle in 316 BC. Despite a number of setbacks, including the Samnites being joined by the Etruscans and Umbri in the north, Rome at length would emerge triumphant in this war. Now, the Roman view was that the optics of war, post-Caudine Forks, was a life or death struggle that could only end in one of two ways. The first was the enemy to cease to be a threat, either because it had become a subordinate ally of Rome, or because it had ceased to exist as a political entity. The only alternative was for Rome itself to cease to exist.

What is in a name?

For all its fame as the site of such a humiliating event, this is the one and only appearance of the Caudine Forks in the historical scene. What is more, the name is variously given as *Furculae Caudinae* (Liv. 9.2.6), *Furcae Caudinae* (Luc. *B civ.* 2.138), and *Caudinae Fauces* (Sil. *Pun.* 8.566).

The term 'forks' is a bit confusing, and to be honest the exact significance of *furculae*, *furcae* or *fauces* is uncertain. One interesting possibility is that it

Piana di Prata, an upland valley running east–west in the middle of the Taburno Camposauro, another of the three alternative locations for the Caudine Forks. We are looking at Monte Camposauro from the northern slopes of Monte Taburno, while the town of Benevento, ancient Beneventum, is just visible in the lowlands to the far right. There is some discrepancy as to which of the Oscan people it belonged: the elder Pliny (*HN* 3.16) assigns it to the Hirpini, whereas Livy (22.13.1) seems to consider it belonged to the Caudini, and Ptolemy (3.1.67) follows suit. (Alfonso Abbatiello/Wikimedia Commons/CC-BY-SA-3.0)

The medieval walls of Sant'Agata de' Goti ('of the Goths'), Campania, the site of the Samnite stronghold of Saticula. The River Isclero runs through the wooded defile below the town as it heads for its confluence with the Volturno, the ancient Volturnus. In 316 BC, the Romans would besiege Saticula, which fell the following year, a Roman success that marked the resumption of hostilities in the Second Samnite War. Two years later, the Romans would plant a Latin colony at Saticula, thereby securing the sensitive region between Caudium, the Caudini stronghold less than 15km away, and Capua down in the Campanian Plain. The cognomen de'Goti is derived from the Hispano-Franc family de Goth, which received the town in fief from Robert d'Anjou, King of Naples (r. 1309–43), the central figure of Italian politics of his day. (Kris de Curtis/Wikimedia Commons/CC-BY-SA-2.0)

is not actually a topographical term such as 'fork in the road' or 'a narrow pass', but may indeed derive from the Latin *furcula*, the diminutive of *furca*, a small two-pronged fork, which has several meaning such as 'wishbone' or 'oxbow'. The latter is of particular interest, for it is the U-shaped wooden or metal frame, a bow, which fits under and around the neck of oxen, with the upper ends inserted through the bar of the bow yoke (Lat. *iugum*), the wooden crosspiece worn by a pair of working oxen. It is a plural noun and is rendered as such both in modern Italian and English, *forche* and 'forks', though in truth it would make more sense to say *giogo* or 'yoke'. In modern Italian there is the expression *le forche Caudine*, as in 'that was his Caudine Forks' – his downfall, his final resounding defeat, his Waterloo, to deploy another appropriate military metaphor.

ANALYSIS

The advent of the paper cartridge, the iron ramrod, smokeless powder, the machine gun, the aircraft, the tank, the computer and the drone have changed the way wars are fought, but not the way they are won. These elements are the hardware of warfare, the basic necessities, important but not decisive. The software of warfare, by contrast, covers anything from generalship and human behaviour to strategy, planning, secrecy, surprise and deception, and indeed the whole array of tactics, trickery and duplicity. As regards this, maximum advantage can be obtained when part of one's own force can get round the enemy to fall upon his rear. To execute such a manoeuvre, secrecy, speed of movement and some way of coordinating the forces on either side of the enemy are necessary: not easy, but most effective if successful.

At the tactical level, the one that really concerns us here, envelopment, places the enemy under severe immediate threat from front and rear, and possibly flank as well. Envelopment has at least four cardinal advantages: first, the *surprise* factor of appearing behind the enemy, both psychological and practical (in that it will take time for the enemy to make arrangements to deal with the new threat); second, reinforcements and supplies are prevented from reaching the enemy; third, his retreat is cut off; and fourth, movement towards the enemy rear is accomplished more economically in terms of casualties and supplies, as one does not have to fight through him but goes round him.

The enemy can also be enveloped from both flanks, called a double envelopment. This is sometimes called the pincer movement, for obvious reasons. Hannibal Barca is considered, quite properly, the finest captain of his day, and the archetype of this movement is, of course, his victory at Cannae in 216 BC. Double envelopment (indeed, single envelopment also) can be achieved either by having one's centre fall back, while the wings remain static, as was the case at Cannae, or by having the centre stand firm and advancing the wings, as at Isandhlwana (24 January 1879) or Khalkhin Gol (20–31 August 1939), and as intended in a single envelopment in the Schlieffen Plan (August 1914). In these well-known examples, however, the encircled enemy fought bitterly and with all the courage of despair. It is clearly for this reason that Sun Tzu suggests that an army should not be completely encircled but should be given some scope for 'a way of escape' (*The Art of War*).

We have just made mention of Count von Schlieffen. He is rightly remembered not only for training the German Army and staff for the

Italy subsequent to the Second Samnite War

Key events

500 BC   Rome defeats Latin coalition forces at Lake Regillus (499 BC or 496 BC).
338 BC   Rome dissolves Latin League.
298 BC   Third Samnite War begins.
290 BC   Peace with Samnites.
272 BC   Rome forms alliance with Thurii, Heraclea and Metapontum; surrender of Taras (renamed Tarentum).
264 BC   First Punic War begins: Roman army lands in Sicily.
218 BC   Second Punic War begins: Latin colonies at Placentia and Cremona; Hannibal Barca in northern Italy;
         Roman army lands in Iberia.

Expansion of Rome

500 BC
338 BC
298 BC
290 BC
272 BC
264 BC
218 BC

DAUNII   Tribes or peoples

0   100 miles
0   100km

CENOMANI   *VENETI*

INSUBRES   Mediolanum   *Gallia*   Verona   *BOII*
                           Cisalpina   Patavium
                              Cremona
TAURINI   *ANARES*   Placentia
                              Parma
LIGURES   *FRINIATES*   Mutina
               Genoa

                              SENONES   Ariminium

Ligurian Sea   Pisae   *AGER*   Ancona
                                  GALLICUS
                          Arretium   Sentium
                                   SABINI   Firmum Picenum
               Populonia   *ETRUSCI* Perusia *PICENI*
                   Vetulonia   Volsinii   *UMBRI*
                                            Spoletium
CARTHAGINIENSES   Cosa   Narnia   *Adriatic Sea*
               Aleria   Tarquinii *LATINS*
                              Veii   *FRENTANI*
                                  Rome
                              Ostia   *APULINI*
                                     SAMNITES   Arpi
                                  Antium   Luceria
                                         VOLSCI   Ausculum
                              Terracina   Capua   *DAUNII*
                                   Neapolis Maloentum Venusia
               Olbia   Salernum   Brundisium
                                                         Tarentum
SARDOS   Paestum Metapontum *MESSAPII*
                                              LUCANI   Heraclea
               Tyrrhenian Sea   Thurii

               Carales
                                              BRUTTII
CARTHAGINIENSES   Croton

                                                   Locri
                                       Messana
                              Panormus   Regium
               CARTHAGINIENSES *GRAECI*
                   Lilybaeum   Agrigentum
                                         Gela   Syracuse

                   Carthage   N
CARTHAGINIENSES

ILLYRIANS

conduct of 'mass warfare', in which it had proved superior to other armies in 1914 and for a long time afterwards, but also in stressing historical experience in developing the concept of the 'battle of annihilation' through encirclement of the enemy, if possible on both flanks. This permeated Schlieffen's entire official and unofficial writings. In developing this point, Schlieffen did what many critics have done in literature and other fields in attributing intentions to the artist which were perhaps not there originally. This was particularly true of Schlieffen's famous study *Cannae*. To return to 321 BC, let us consider if this has any relevance to the events that unfolded at Caudine Forks.

If the enemy is completely prevented from withdrawing, which may also have the effect of preventing reinforcements or supplies reaching him, he is said to be encircled. An encircled enemy does not have to be completely surrounded by an unbroken cordon of troops: it is sufficient simply to cut off his lines of retreat and resupply, which can be done with relatively small groups of forces. This was in all probability the situation at the Caudine Forks. After all, the likes of narrow defiles and mountain forests are often the means by which a few can overcome the many.

AMBUSH

Clausewitz goes so far as to say that the element of surprise 'lies at the root of all operations without exception, though in widely varying degrees, depending on the nature and circumstances of the operation' (*Vom Krieg*). On many occasions, surprise is deliberately included with the aid of deception,

Panoramic view of Terracina, Lazio, looking northwards to the promontory of Monte Circeo. In the middle distance the Volscian Hills descend to the edge of the narrow coastal strip on which Terracina is situated. The Volscian settlement of Anxur was finally secured by the Romans in 329 BC with the establishment of a *colonia maritima civium*. Renamed Tarracina, the colony commanded the Pomptinae (Pontine) Marshes: *urbs prona paludes*, 'a city surrounded by marshes', as Livy (4.59.4) calls it. In 315 BC to the north-east of the colony was fought the Battle of Lautulae, the second major Samnite victory during the Second Samnite War. Roman historians would rewrite the outcome of the battle as inconclusive, but the truth is the Romans suffered one of the heaviest defeats of the war. (Ra Boe/Wikimedia Commons/ CC-BY-SA-3.0)

which ensures that the attack is not anticipated. Deception and surprise are two key principles.

'Now war is based on deception', opined Sun Tzu. A skilled commander must be master of the complementary arts of simulation and dissimulation. One example will illustrate his point. Red Force uses deception to mislead Blue Force with regard to its real intentions and capabilities. By deploying deception, Red Force will try to cause Blue Force to act in ways that will eventually prove prejudicial to it. Naturally, Red Force will hope Blue Force will realize this deception only when it is too late for it to react. An example of this is the classic ambush, in which the concealment of the attackers (viz. Red Force) and secrecy surrounding the attack provide the deception. In an ambush, therefore, a force (viz. Blue Force) is frequently decoyed into a trap as it is lured past the concealed foe, which will then break cover and launch an attack in flank and rear. The psychological impact of surprise may paralyze the thoughts and actions of the ambushed, leaving them incapable of reacting effectively. Secrecy is thus the absolutely essential element for success in all ambushes. And so it proved at the Caudine Forks.

As any modern soldier knows, an ambush is a surprise attack, by a force lying in wait, upon a moving or temporarily halted enemy. It is usually a brief encounter and does not require the capture and holding of ground. Almost invariably the action will take place at close range, the aim being to paralyze the ambushed through shock. There are two types of ambush, namely deliberate (by design) and immediate (by an inspiration of the moment). The first type is planned and executed as an independent operation. Frequently, it will be easier to achieve success with a small ambush rather than a large one, and in modern warfare this will be carried out by infantry up to platoon size. The second type is one set with a minimum of planning to anticipate imminent enemy action. The total success of its execution relies on the initiative and agility of the commander and the ability and discipline of his men.

Gola dell'Isclero and the narrow valley between Sant'Agata de' Goti and Moiano, along which runs the River Isclero. We are looking north-east towards Monte Taburno, its upper slopes obscured by cloud. Some scholars suggest that the Caudine Forks are to be sought here. The location does seem to answer best to Livy's description *via alia per cavam rupem*, 'by one road through the rocky defile' (9.2.9). However, there is one grave objection to this being the actual location of the ambush site: in 321 BC, the Valle Moiano was dominated by the Samnite stronghold of Saticula. (Decan/Wikimedia Commons/ CC-BY-SA-4.0)

Speaking from personal experience, in selecting a killing area – that is to say, the location where you intend to achieve your mission – you want terrain in which obviously the enemy force is going to enter; it has ground that can channel the enemy force; and is spacious enough so that the ambush force can destroy the enemy. It is possible the ability of Gavius Pontius to use terrain to best advantage, as he clearly did at the Caudine Forks, derived from an innate appreciation of it.

Surprise and ambush are, of course, linked together; an ambush, after all, depends on surprise being achieved. Surprise is twofold; that is, surprise brought about by doing something that the enemy does not expect (moral surprise), and surprise brought about by doing something that the enemy cannot counter (material surprise). Similarly, simplicity in your planning is a must. As in any military plan, it must be clear and concise. Each element conducting the ambush must understand completely its purpose and its task. Too many moving parts are *not* an option. Finally, a detailed knowledge of the enemy is vital, as it will influence the plan and should include the likely enemy method of movement. In this respect, an ambush is optimally laid on the most probable route of advance of the enemy. And so it proved, once again, at the Caudine Forks.

When it comes to positioning the ambush, the site selected should be easy to conceal, so that from an enemy point of view it appears unoccupied. In other words, the ambush is invisible. Despite the recommendation of Sun Tzu on this particular matter, there should be *no* offer of an easy escape out of the killing area once the ambush has been sprung. The location should be such that it allows lookouts timely warning before the first enemy enter the killing area. It should have a good covered approach avoiding contact

A well-preserved stretch of the Via Appia at Sant'Andrea, kilometre 126, Parco Naturale dei Monti Aurunci. The construction of the Via Appia in 312 BC added to the strategic importance of the Roman colony of Tarracina; it was here at the southern tip of Latium that the road first touched on the sea. Initially the main roadway from Rome to Campania, the Romans would push the Via Appia to the Adriatic port of Brundisium (Brindisi) in 264 BC, an important travel node as one of the usual ports for sea travel to Greece and beyond. The Via Appia, and those that came after, appears to have formalized many of the ancient routes already apparently in use. It must be said that the celebrated, well-preserved, basalt-paved Roman roads stretching for miles do not belong to our period of study; they are typically the product of the Roman principate. (Carole Raddato/Flickr/ CC-BY-SA-2.0)

Funerary art (Paestum, Museo Archeologico Nazionale di Paestum), Necropoli di Andriuolo, Tomba 114, Lastra Nord, dated *c.* 330/320 BC. A battle scene with realistic or possibly even historical content, as it depicts two Greek-style phalanxes about to crunch into one another against a backdrop of mountains. The one on the right is believed to be the winning side, as it is led by a figure, heroically nude apart from his bronze-faced *clipeus* and bronze helmet adorned with a red crest and black feathers. He is in the act of thrusting with his spear, and is perhaps to be identified with the pan-Italic Mamers/Mars, the twin side feathers being emblematic of the war god (Vir. *Aen.* 6.779, Val. Max. 1.8.6). Noteworthy are the individual blazons on the *clipî*. It should be kept in mind, however, out of a thousand burials spanning the entire 4th century BC, only 80 bear pictorial decoration, and 50 of these lay in the urban necropolises, mainly in that of Andriuolo. (© Esther Carré)

with the enemy or local inhabitants. As the commander cannot see the whole of his command, the need for maintaining concealment, and the absence of movement, noise and smell whilst in hiding, is an absolute must. Ultimately, a cleverly concealed ambush will not only achieve surprise but also catch the enemy when he is least expecting to be ambushed. Surprise is paramount.

In sum, the purpose of an ambush is not to hold a piece of ground. It is to destroy the enemy as a fighting force, be it physically or psychologically. The ground is used to achieve the ambush, but the ground itself is not what the ambusher is fighting for. So, there were two ways in which, when it came to facing the consular armies of Rome, Gavius Pontius could handle it. He might choose a strong position across their line of march, thus challenging them to a pitched battle. Obviously, in such a scenario he would take unnecessary casualties. But another plan was open to Gavius Pontius. He would follow the dictum 'be deceptive' and thereby outwit his enemy by encircling and entrapping the consular armies where they were stretched out in a long column of route at a location lacking in sufficient room to manoeuvre. It is in a tight spot that an army on the march can be isolated and demoralized; its will to resist broken. Thus, without battle it can be conquered. However, to do so takes patience, discipline and good timing.

CONCLUSION

When you travel down the long length of peninsular Italy, be it along the west coast or the east, you soon realize that it is a country where much of the terrain offers an endless series of obstacles to an invading army. Below the rich alluvial plains of the Po Valley one quickly finds one great mountain range, the only low ground being the narrow coastal strips and the river valleys which fan out from the central spine like spindly fish bones. It is for this reason that we should give adequate attention to the serious restrictions on movement imposed by the peninsula's mountains and rivers.

We have already noted that the Second Samnite War was one of attrition. It is plausible, even if it cannot be proved, that the eclipse of the Greek-style phalanx from the Roman battlefield and the introduction of the three-line manipular legion may have been learned through bitter necessity and hard experience, fighting in the rough, rocky terrain of the interior of central Italy, a region dominated by the Apennines, during this protracted, bruising conflict. As Arnold Toynbee (1965, 1.505–18) once observed, military reforms often followed great defeats. It is of course arguable that it was the

The Via Appia passing through the Forum Aemilianum in Terracina. Begun in 312 BC and named after Appius Claudius Caedus, the censor of that year, this was the first of the great Roman roads. It is attested that the Via Appia was originally a plain gravel road, and its paving was progressively improved during the 3rd century BC. (MM/Wikimedia Commons/ Public Domain)

The shape, size, weight and the way it was employed came in numerous forms, yet the spear was used in two ways: throwing or thrusting. The wealthiest citizen soldiers of archaic Rome stood in the foremost ranks of the phalanx and wielded the *hasta*, a long thrusting spear. This 5th-century BC Etruscan bronze spearhead (Arezzo, Museo Archeologico Nazionale di Arezzo) once formed the business end of a *hasta*. It has a leaf-shaped blade with a midrib and ends in a closed socket (note the small hole which would have had a nail driven through it into the ashen shaft). The midrib gives greater longitudinal strength to a spearhead, increasing its effectiveness at piercing shields and body armour. In the tight confines of the phalanx, the *hasta* would have been used in a jabbing manner by those stationed in the first two ranks. (© Esther Carré).

events of 390 BC that marked the watershed moment in early Roman history, this being the point in time identified by Livy as the 'second birth' (*secunda origine*, 6.1) of Rome. Conversely, if we were to choose between the greater threats to Rome's existence as a powerful polity in central Italy, then in all likelihood it would be the Samnites and not the Gauls. The literary sources offer us two contrasting pictures of how significant Rome's troubles with the Gauls were in the 4th century BC, with Polybios (2.18–35) implying that the Gaulish incursions from the north were part of a larger effort to settle, while Livy indicates that the Gauls were raiders seeking portable wealth, particularly cattle and slaves, as their main objective, even if he (5.36.3) does note on one occasion land was one of the spoils of war sought by them.

Theoretically indestructible from the front, the Greek-style phalanx was indeed a formidable weapon. Yet it did have two distinct disadvantages. First, it was not flexible, and once locked into the mêlée, it was unable to turn abruptly to face a threat to its unprotected flanks or rear. Second, it required level, open terrain for its cohesion. So, the way of the phalanx had lain on the coastal plain – like the great coastal plain of Latium – and a war waged in the constricted terrain of the mountainous spine of central Italy meant the citizen soldiers of Rome were constantly at the mercy of ambuscades, supply failures, missed rendezvous or the rash overstretching of the line of march. Little wonder, therefore, the Romans came to be embarrassed at the Caudine Forks, as they were again six years later – 315 BC – at the defile of Lautulae (Passo di Portello) just north-east of the colony of Tarracina (Terracina), where the coastal route (later consolidated as the Via Appia) between Latium and Campania was narrow, shut in between the Volscian Hills and the Tyrrhenian Sea (Liv. 9.23.4–6, Diod. Sic. 19.72.6–7). The Samnites did well in mobile warfare, and we may safely surmise they had a long tradition of using mountain ambushes against invaders. The very worst thing they could do was to go down to the flat lands and face their more conventional Roman foe there.

The Roman phalanx, with its advantage of brute strength, might defeat the mountain men of Samnium on the level plain, but once they had to be tackled amid the broken ground of their homeland, they would present the Romans with a stiffer problem. So little is known of these years of mountain warfare, hidden as they are in the womb of time, but history knows few, if any, places of education as unforgiving as the red field of battle; thus, there can be little doubt that the Romans learned more pliant tactics when it came to the topographic realities of Samnium. Anyone who chooses may quarrel with this argument (q.v. Lendon 2009, pp. 190–92). In spite of that, the next logical step is to consider the Roman adoption of the *pilum* and the *scutum*, the first armament, if not both, indubitably changing the tactics of the legion.

LEARNING FROM THE ENEMY

It is of course likely that both these two pieces of war gear may have been linked tactically. The legion was essentially a development of the phalanx, which the Romans articulated into three lines, *triplex acies*, with each line in turn broken up into small blocks capable of independent manoeuvre, and with enough elbow room between soldiers to allow them to use their weapons effectively. It is said, for instance by Diodorus Siculus, among others:

CARCERE MAMERTINO
E
SOTTERRANEO TVLLIANO

QVI PERIRONO VITTIME
DEI TRIONFI DI ROMA

PONZIO RE DEI SANNITI
GIÀ VINCITORE ALLE FORCHE CAVDINE
DECAPITATO   AN.290 A.C.
QVINTO PLEMINIO GIÀ GOVERNATORE DI LOCRI
SVPPLIZIATO   AN.180 A.C.
I SEGVACI DEI GRACCHI VINDICI DELLA PLEBE
STRANGOLATI   AN.123 A.C.
GIVGVRTA RE DI NVMIDIA
MORTO PER FAME AN.104 A.C.
ARISTOBVLO II RE DEI GIVDEI
DECAPITATO   AN. 61 A.C.
LENTVLO E CETEGO SENATORI ROMANI
E ALTRI COMPLICI DI CATILINA
STRANGOLATI   AN. 60 A.C.
VERCINGETORICE RE DELLA GALLIA
DECAPITATO   AN. 49 A.C.
SEIANO MINISTRO DI TIBERIO
DECAPITATO   AN. 31 D.C.
SIMONE DI GIORA DIFENSORE DI GERVSALEMME
CONTRO TITO E VESPASIANO
DECAPITATO   AN. 70 D.C.

E MOLTI ALTRI OSCVRI O MENO ILLVSTRI
CADVTI TRA I GORGHI
DEGLI ODII E DEGLI EVENTI VMANI

Marble plaque in the Carcere Mamertino, Capitoline Hill, Rome, naming some of the more illustrious inmates and listing how and when each one died. In Italian we can read PONZIO RE DEI SANNITI / GIA VINCITORE ALLE FORCHE CAVDINE / DECAPITATO AN.290 A.C, 'Pontius king of the Samnites, victor of the Caudine Forks, beheaded 290 BC'. In Roman times the dungeon was known as the Tullianum, and its two subterranean cells, one on top of the other, held criminals and captives awaiting their execution. The lower cell was located within the sewer system and could only be reached by being lowered through a hole in the floor of the upper cell. Sallust describes it 'as disgusting and vile by reason of the filth, darkness and stench' (*Cat.* 55.4). Such was the awful end of Gavius Pontius, hero of the Second Samnite War. (Lalupa/Wikimedia Commons/CC-BY-SA-3.0)

The Etruscans, who fought in phalanxes with round shields of bronze [χαλκαῖς ἀσπίσι], compelled [the Romans] to adopt similar arms and, consequently, were defeated. Then, when other peoples were using shields [viz. *scuta*] such as the Romans now use, and were fighting in maniples, they imitated both and so overcame the originators of such fine models. (Diod. Sic. 23.2.1)

Yet this is an unsophisticated and transparent argument that plays up the native Italic tradition. In all probability, this major organizational and tactical change owes its origins to the Italiote *poleis* that dotted the coastlines of southern Italy and eastern Sicily. All the same, either Etruscan- or Greek-inspired, the adoption of mass fighting in tight formation, mustering a militia army organized around a phalanx composed of citizens wealthy enough to outfit themselves with the complete panoply of an armoured spearman, was

ABOVE: The splendid finds (Rome, Museo Nazionale Romano, Terme di Diocleziano, inv. 115194–1151207) from the Tomba del Guerriero di Lanuvio, Lazio, ancient Lanuvium, dated *c.* 480 BC. The war gear includes a bronze muscle-corselet (with traces of leather and linen), broad bronze belt, bronze Negau helmet (with eyes in glass paste, silver and gold), iron spearheads and an iron *kopis.* This panoply would have been worn by a citizen in the foremost ranks of the phalanx. The athletic equipment includes a bronze discus, two iron strigils and an alabastra for olive oil, a fitting reminder of the dual aristocratic pursuits of war and sport. **BELOW:** Italic Negau helmet and Etruscan greave (Ravenna, Museo Nazionale di Ravenna), Necropoli di San Martino, Tomba 10, both of bronze, 5th century BC. Albeit Umbrian in context, such equipment would not look out of place in the Servian phalanx of archaic Rome. The use of Italic armour, in this case the wide-brimmed pot helmet, hardly affected the tactical function of the Greek-style phalanx as long as the front-rank citizen soldiers bore the *clipeus* and *hasta*. Negau helmets and greaves are often found together. (Above – Ursus/Wikimedia Commons/ Public Domain; Below – © Esther Carré)

radical. It was, after all, antithetical to the highly individualistic mode of warfare utilized in low-level raiding over short distances.

As for those 'other peoples' in Diodoros' passage, they have often been interpreted by modern commentators as the Samnites. If the Romans indeed had changed their weapons and tactics under the influence of their brutal confrontations with the Samnites, the most obvious stimulus for such a step would have been a major military reverse. During the Second Samnite War,

there were at least two of these that we know of for certain: the Caudine Forks and the Battle of Lautulae.

The next step in the development of the Roman army, which falls after the regal period and in the early Republic, is associated traditionally with the name of Marcus Furius Camillus, a national hero credited with saving recently sacked Rome from the Gauls and commemorated as a second founder of Rome. Anyway, these military reforms fall under three headings: first, the introduction of a daily cash allowance, the *stipendium*, for soldiers; second, the adoption of the *scutum* instead of the *clipeus* as the standard shield, while the *pilum* was substituted for the *hasta*; and finally, the abolishment of the phalanx to be replaced by the manipular legion, two in number, each of 3,000 legionaries, each commanded by a consul (Liv. 1.43.1, 5.7.5, 8.8.3, Plut. *Cam.* 40.3–4). In turn, Dionysios of Halikarnassos has Camillus give a speech to his soldiers praising their 'sturdy oblong shields' (θυρεοί/*thureoi*) which offer protection to the whole body, and a replacement of the spear with 'a long javelin [λόγχης ʽυσσός/*lógkhês hyssós*] against which there is no protection' (*Ant. Rom.* 14.9.2).

That all these major changes were effected at the same time and under the guidance of one quasi-legendary man is in itself improbable. Though the multi-year siege of Veii may well have necessitated the provision of remuneration to allow the citizen soldiers to meet their basic living expenses while away from home for an increasingly lengthy period – an innovation, if it really did happen at this time, which would go well with the transition from seasonal raiding warfare to year-round campaigns – the adoption of new equipment and a new tactical formation is much more likely the result of experience gained from a series of campaigns over a long period of time.

Tomba dei Rilievi, Necropoli della Banditaccia, Cerveteri, Lazio. Known by the Romans as Caere, this was the Etruscan urban state of Caisra. Discovered in 1847, the late 4th-century BC or early 3rd-century BC Etruscan tufa-cut tomb (hypogeum) is highly decorated with painted stucco bas-reliefs instead of the more common frescoes. These cover the walls and pillars of the tomb chamber itself. According to an inscription within, this tomb belonged to the Matuna *lautun* (Lat. *gens*), members of which served as magistrates in Caisra. Their martial prowess is shown by the eclectic collection of life-sized helmets, armour, shields and weapons, which are depicted in the reliefs as if stowed by hanging them from pegs. (Roberto Ferrari/Wikimedia Commons/CC-BY-SA-2.0)

When it came to the grim business of war, the notion of borrowing military hardware (and often improving upon its forms) from other peoples was unproblematic to the pragmatic and adaptable Romans. This was one of their strong points, and, as Polybios properly points out, 'no people are more willing to adopt new customs and to emulate what they see is better done by others' (6.25.10). According to a senatorial speech Sallust puts into the mouth of a thirty-something Iulius Caesar, the Romans *arma atque tela militaria ab Samnitibus*, 'borrowed most of their armour and throwing weapons from the Samnites' (*Cat.* 51.38). And yet Sallust unfortunately does not clarify his statement by actually naming the armour or the throwing weapons, though the former may have been *scuta* and the latter *pila*.

One thing we can be certain of is the fact that the Romans inherited the *pilum*, like most of their war gear, from one of the peoples whom they met on the battlefield, and over time developed it from a more rudimentary weapon to make it their own. As the exiled Augustan poet Ovid points out, *fas est et ab hoste doceri*, 'one should learn even from one's enemies' (*Met.* 4.428, cf. Poly. 6.25.11). In the Livian legion, there is no reference to the *pilum*, which, if Livy's narrative is accepted, may not yet have been introduced. The earliest reference to the *pilum* actually belongs to 293 BC during the Third Samnite War (Liv. 10.39.12, cf. Plut. *Pyrr.* 21.9), though the earliest authentic use of this weapon may belong to 251 BC (Polyb. 1.40.12, υσσός/ *hyssós* in his Greek). Following this one hypothesis advocates that the *pilum* was forged on an Iberian model, what the Romans called the *falarica* (e.g. Liv. 21.8.10–12). In this case, the weapon may have been seen first in the hands of Iberian mercenaries employed by the Carthaginians during the First

Pair of Etruscan greaves (New York, Metropolitan Museum of Art, invs. 22.139.12 & 22.139.13) of bronze, 4th century BC. The hardest parts of the body to protect with the shield were the lower legs, and, although not in itself fatal, a blow to the shins could prove debilitating enough to allow the soldier's guard to slip, thus opening him for a killing blow. Though cumbersome to wear, greaves covered the knee and reached down to the ankle, following the musculature of the calf, thereby clipping neatly round the lower legs by their own elasticity. We must assume, therefore, that they were custom-made for the owner, fitting the individual shape and length of his lower legs. Additionally, they were clearly made in mirror form for the right and left lower legs. (Metropolitan Museum of Art/ Wikimedia Commons/CC0 1.0)

Punic War (264–241 BC). As for the Italic oval shield, the *scutum*, this was already being carried by some of the soldiers at this date, while some of them continued to be armed with the *hasta* for 200 years or more. When all is said and done, it is likely that a whole bunch of piecemeal reforms were later lumped together and attributed to the wisdom of Camillus, who, after all, was the period's most famous general.

The most explicit version of the potential origin of the *pilum* can be found in the *Ineditum Vaticanum*, a Greek treatise of unknown authorship conceivably from the 2nd century BC, which attributes the Samnites with introducing the weapon, as well as the oval *scutum*, to the Roman army (von Arnim 1892). It is probably for this reason that the *pilum* sometimes gets called a Sabellian weapon (Virg. *Aen.* 7.665) or the *iaculator Sabellus* (Sil. *Pun.* 4.221). Conversely, the 2nd-century AD collector of anecdotes, the convivial Athenaios (6.273f), says that while the *scutum* was adopted during the Samnite wars, the *pilum* was acquired from the Iberians. There is no evidence any of the Oscans ever used this weapon, but the elder Pliny (*HN* 7.291) attributes the invention of the *pilum* to the Etruscans, which does at least place the origin of this throwing weapon within the Italian Peninsula. In support of Pliny is the funerary painting in the late 4th-century BC Tomba Giglioli, Necropolis of Tarquinia, which depicts three likely *pila*-like weapons between two *clipî*. Weapons of this type were also used by the Senonian Gauls, for a number of socketed iron shanks with different types of head, all dated to the end of the 4th century BC, were discovered in the Montefortino necropolis (Small 2000, pp. 225–26). The earliest archaeological examples of what are almost certainly Roman *pila* are known from Talamonaccio (Bishop 2017, p. 12). This was ancient Telamon, the dramatic scene of a decisive victory over a coalition of Cisalpina Gauls in 225 BC; they may have been deposited as a votive offering in a local temple.

Military changes, however, rarely occur in response to the simple arrival of a new technology, but are instead dictated by a range of socio-political principles which actually favour conservatism over innovation. Notably, it has been said by critics of the military profession that 'peacetime generals always fight the last war'; that is, all armies, regardless of when we are talking about, are basically using the lessons learned from the last war in the hopes of winning the next one. The point is well made, for military leaders do tend to have their feet firmly planted in the past. So the ambiguity and confusion in our literary sources is most likely explained by the fact that the transition in Roman military hardware, although most likely a response to new stimuli, was not swift but almost certainly slow. Alternatively, of course, the Romans did not know the true origins of the *pilum* or the *scutum*.

Curiously, the *Ineditum Vaticanum* does not make mention of the *gladius*, which in a later period would be the sword par excellence of the Roman army. It is believed that sometime in the 3rd century BC the Romans adopted a long-pointed, double-edged Iberian weapon, which they called the *gladius Hispaniensis*, 'Iberian sword'. A later lexicographer, possibly following Polybios' lost account of the Iberian war, says the *gladius Hispaniensis* (Gk. Ιβερικός/ *Iberikós*) was adopted from the Iberians (or Celtiberians) at the time of the war with Hannibal, but it is possible that this weapon, along with *pilum*, was adopted from those aforementioned Iberian mercenaries in the pay of Carthage (Polyb. fr. 179 with Walbank 1957, p. 704, cf. Bishop 2017, pp. 7–8).

JUST IN TIME FOR HANNIBAL

The restructuring of these tactical formations from the larger, inflexible phalanx to the more manoeuvrable blocks meant this reform of the Roman army represented a radical change in terms of deployment of a legion. However, our literary sources disagree about when exactly the Romans made this reform, although most place it in the 4th century BC. On the other hand, as opposed to one radical change, we should perhaps understand the adoption of a more articulated organizational system as a series of gradual changes. For instance, even in the 2nd century BC one element of the Roman army (the *triarii*) still acted in a manner that was similar to the Greek-style phalanx, or so it appears.

By the time of the war with Hannibal, most legionaries were armed with *pila* and *gladii* (albeit in the latter's proto-form), but the third line still retained the *hasta*. These blocks, the *manipuli*, 'handfuls', derived from the handful of straw suspended from a pole as a military standard and, hence, soldiers belonging to the same unit. Each *manipulus* was made up of two *centuriae*, centuries, the administrative sub-units each under a *centurio* and an *optio*, and each identified by its own standard, *signum*. The *manipulus* therefore was the basic tactical unit in the Roman battleline and was under the command of the *centurio prior*, the senior of the two centurions and leader of the right-hand *centuria* (or front), unless he was *hors de combat*, in which case the junior, *centurio posterior*, took command. The result of the maniple was a more tactically versatile, yet inherently demanding, organization.

Yet (to repeat), the Romans sacrificed the depth and cohesion of the phalanx for mobility and flexibility, the latter being the essential ingredient. It was not until this articulation was achieved that deployments and tactics became malleable elements which could be planned to fit the needs.[6] In this way, a Roman commander could send in the maniples of the first two lines to attack in turn, the legionaries casting their *pila* and running to meet the enemy head-on with their *gladii*. Their *scuta* often themselves served as offensive weapons, as legionaries punched their metal bosses against the bodies of the enemy. In their combined use of *pilum*, *scutum* and *gladius*, the defining pieces of war gear for a legionary, the Romans had partially solved the age-old tactical dilemma of choosing between missile and shock attack. For the Romans, firepower meant

6   Conversely, Armstrong (*Early Roman Warfare*, 2016, p. 102, cf. pp. 150–53) argues that the maniples 'were the descendants of the archaic war bands of the 5th century BC'; that is, an aggregation of these archaic Roman formations.

pilum-power. Thus, at the turn of the 2nd century BC, the soldier poet Quintus Ennius (d. 169 BC) could write from experience: *Hastati spargunt hastas; fit ferreus imber*, 'the *hastati* hurl their *hastae*; an iron downpour came' (*Ann.* 8. fr. 281 Vahlen).[7]

At ranges of 15m or less, a withering volley of *pila* was in the highest degree murderous, undermining the impact of an enemy assault by disorganizing their foremost ranks. Unsurprisingly, the question that immediately comes to mind is if the *hastati*, 'spearmen', carry *pila*, why does Ennius have them hurling *hastae*, thrusting spears? Fashioned out of ash wood and some 2–2.5m in length, this ashen spear was equipped with a bronze or iron spearhead. The weapon was usually thrust over arm in a jabbing motion, the spear tip to the face of the foe, although it could easily be thrust underarm if the spearman was charging into contact at the run. The centre of the shaft was bound in cord or rawhide for a secure grip. This armament was certainly not thrown. So, to return to the question posed above. First, a simple matter of poetical alliteration on Ennius' part; and second, *hastati* were originally armed with *hastae*, as Varro (*Ling.* 5.89) makes clear, before being re-equipped with *pila* – much like grenadiers were still called grenadiers long after they had abandoned their eponymous grenades.

Prior to putting down his *pilum* to pick up the pen, Ennius had served in the Roman army with the rank of centurion during the war with Hannibal. The epic poet Silius Italicus describes the duel between centurion Ennius and Prince Hostus, son of Hampsagoras (Livy's Hampsicora), leader of the Sardo-Punic aristocracy, during the Sardinian rebellion of 215 BC:

> Foremost in the fight was Ennius, a scion of the ancient stock of King Messapus [*antique Messapi ab origine regis*]; and his right hand the vine-staff [*vitis*], the distinguishing badge of the Roman centurion. He came from the rugged land of Calabria, and he was a son of ancient Rudiae – Rudiae which now owes all her

---

7   The line received the accolade of being quoted by Virgil (*Aen.* 12.284).

fame to this child of hers. He fought in the van [*miscebat primas acies*]; and, even as the Thracian bard [Orpheus, one of the Argonauts] long ago dropped his lyre and hurled missiles brought from Rhodope, when Cyzicus made war upon the Argo, so Ennius had made himself conspicuous by slaying many of the enemy, and his ardour in battle grew with the number of his victims. Now, hoping to win everlasting fame by disposing of such a dangerous foe, Hostus flew at Ennius and strongly hurled his spear [*ac perlibrat viribus hastam*]. (Sil. *Pun.* 12.393–404 Duff, cf. Liv. 23.40.3–4, 23.41.3–4)

In short, the spear is sent wide by the intervention of Apollo, protector of poets, who then slays Hostus with an avenging arrow, so sparing the life of the young poet at war so that he 'shall be the first to sing of Roman wars in noble verse' (Sil. *Pun.* 12.410). Ennius was certainly the first Roman to write a narrative of Rome's history in Latin, notwithstanding in hexameter verse yet epic poetry worthy of Apollo.[8]

At this point, mention should be made of elbow room, and in that respect we should note that a *pilum* cannot be effectively used by legionaries standing shoulder to shoulder and shields overlapping as in the monolithic Greek-style phalanx. On the contrary, in the manipular legion there was ample room to aim and hurl the *pilum* – there was no run-up prior to launch, just a standing throw, left foot forward, right foot back (Bishop 2017, p. 46). However, in order to give each man space to use his weapons, he would have, if we are to believe the testimony of Polybios (18.30.5–8), a frontage of 6 Roman feet (1.8m) as well as an equivalent depth. On the other hand, Vegetius (*Mil.* 3.14, 3.15), who appears to be using the elder Cato as his primary source, claims the individual legionaries occupy a frontage of 3 Roman feet (0.9m) with a depth of 6 Roman feet (1.8m) between ranks. However, the retention of the *hasta* as the offensive arm of the *triarii* at the rear shows that the Romans were not yet entirely convinced of the superiority of the *pilum* in all tactical circumstances, but preferred still to depend on the thrusting spear for the final push in the attack, and conversely, in the event of the need for a last stand, hence the adage *rem ad triarios redisse*, 'it has come to the *triarii*' (Liv. 8.8.11).

8   According to Aulus Gellius, Ennius actually spoke three languages, 'Greek, Oscan and Latin', calling them his *tria corda*, 'three hearts' (*NA* 17.17.1); that is, he considered his triple linguistic and cultural heritage as a core part of his identity.

FURTHER READING

Ardant du Picq, C. (trans. Col. J. Greely and Maj. R. Cotton), *Battle Studies: Ancient and Modern*, Harrisburg, PA: U.S. Army War College, 1920, repr. 1946

Armstrong, J., *Early Roman Warfare: From the Regal Period to the First Punic War*, Barnsley: Pen and Sword Military, 2016A

Armstrong, J., *War and Society in Early Rome: From Warlords to Generals*, Cambridge: Cambridge University Press, 2016B

Arnim, von, H., '«Inedtum Vaticanum»'. *Hermes* 27/1, 1892, pp. 118–30

Biondo, F., *Roma Ristaurata, et Italia Illustrata di Biondo da Forlì: Tradotte in Buona Lingua Volgare per Lucio Fauno*, Venezia, 1548

Bishop, M.C., *The Pilum: The Roman Heavy Javelin*, Oxford: Osprey Publishing, 2017

Bispham, E.H., 'The Samnites', in G.J. Bradley, E. Isayev and C. Riva (eds.), *Ancient Italy: Regions without Boundaries*, Exeter: University of Exeter Press, 2007, pp. 179–223

Brizzi, G., *Il guerriero, l'oplita, il legionario*, Bologna: Il Mulino, 2008

Casali, S., 'The Poet at War: Ennius on the Field in Silius' *Punica*', *Arethusa* 39/3, 2006, pp. 569–93

Cascarino, G., *L'Esercito Romano: Armamento e Organizzazione*, Vol. 1: *Dalle origini alla fine della republica*, Rimini: Il Cerchio Iniziative Editoriali, 2007

Cipriani, M., Greco, E., Longo, F. and Pontrandolfo, A., *I Lucani a Pæstum*, Paestum: Fondazione Pæstum, 1996

Connolly, P., *Greece and Rome at War*, Mechanicsburg, PA: Stackpole, 1981 (reprinted 1988, 1998)

Cornell, T.J., 'The recovery of Rome', in F.W Walbank, A.E. Austin, M.W. Frederiksen, R.M. Ogilvie and A. Drummond (eds.), *The Cambridge Ancient History*, Vol. 7, Part 2: *The Rise of Rome to 220* BC, Cambridge: Cambridge University Press, 1990, pp. 309–50

——, *The Beginning of Rome: Italy and Rome from the Bronze Age to the Punic Wars (c. 1000–264 BC)*, London: Routledge, 1995

Cowan, R.H., *Roman Conquest: Italy*, Barnsley: Pen & Sword Military, 2009

——, 'The Samnite *Pilum*: Evidence for the Roman Boasts', *Ancient Warfare*, 6/4, 2012, pp. 39–41

Dench, E., *From Barbarians to New Men: Greek, Roman, and Modern Perceptions of Peoples from the Central Apennines*, Oxford: Clarendon Press, 1995

Fields, N., *Roman Battle Tactics 390–110* BC, Oxford: Osprey Publishing (Elite 172), 2010

——, *Early Roman Warrior 753–321* BC, Oxford: Osprey Publishing (Warrior 156), 2011

——, *Roman Republican Legionary 298–105* BC, Oxford: Osprey Publishing (Warrior 162), 2012

Forsythe, G., *A Critical History of Early Rome*, Berkeley/Los Angeles, CA: University of California Press, 2006

——, 'The Army and the Centuriate Organization in Early Rome', in P. Erdkamp (ed.), *A Companion to the Roman Army*, Oxford: John Wiley & Sons (Blackwell Companions to the Ancient World), 2007, pp. 24–41

Griffith, S.B. (trans.), *Sun Tzu: The Art of War*, Oxford: Oxford University Press, 1963 (reprinted 1971)

Harris, W.V., *War and Imperialism in Republican Rome 327–70* BC, Oxford: Clarendon Press, 1986

Head, D., *Armies of the Macedonian and Punic Wars 359–146* BC, Goring-by-Sea: Wargames Research Group, 1982

Horsfall, N., 'The Caudine Forks: Topography and Illusion', *Papers of the British School of Rome*, 50, 1982, pp. 45–52

Koon, S., *Infantry Combat in Livy's Battle Narratives*, Oxford: BAR Publishing (BAR International Series, 2071), 2010

La Rocca, E., 'Fabio e Fannio: L'Affresco Medio-Repubblicano dell'Esquilino come Riflesso dell'Arte Rappresentativa e come Espressione di Mobilità Sociale', *Dialoghi di Archeologia*, 3, 1984, pp. 31–53

Le Bohec, Y., 'L'Armement des Romains pendant les Guerres Puniques d'après les Sources Littéraires, l'Équipement Militaire et l'Armement de la République', *Journal of Roman Military Equipment Studies*, 8, 1997, pp. 13–24

——, 'Roman Wars and Armies in Livy', in B. Mineo (ed.), *A Companion to Livy*, Oxford: John Wiley & Sons (Blackwell Companions to the Ancient World), 2015, pp. 114–24

Lendon, J.E., *Soldiers and Ghosts: A History of Battle in Classical Antiquity*, New Haven, CT: Yale University Press, 2009

Lomas, K., 'Greeks, Romans, and Others: Problems of Colonialism and Ethnicity in Southern Italy', in J. Webster, and N.J. Cooper (eds.), *Roman Imperialism: Post-Colonial Perspectives*, Leicester: Leicester School of Archaeological Studies (Leicester Archaeology Monographs 3), 1996, pp. 135–44

——, *The Rise of Rome: From the Iron Age to the Punic Wars*, Cambridge, MA: Belknap Press, 2018

Lumsden, A.R., «Ante bella punica»: *Western Mediterranean Military Development 350–264* BC, MA thesis, University of Auckland, 2016

Miles, G.B., *Livy: Reconstructing Early Rome*, Ithaca, NY: Cornell University Press, 1997

Montague, J.D., *Greek and Roman Warfare: Battles, Tactics and Trickery*, London: Greenhill Books, 2006

Oakley, S.P., *The Hill-Forts of the Samnites*, London: British School at Rome, 1995

——, *A Commentary on Livy, Books VI–X*, 4 vols, Oxford: Oxford University Press, 1997–2005

Pontrandolfo, A., Rouveret, A. and Cipriani, M., *Le Tombe Dipinte di Paestum*, Paestum: Fondazione Pæstum, 1998

Rawlings, L.P., 'Celt, Spaniards, and Samnites: Warriors in a Soldiers' War', in T.J. Cornell, N.B. Rankov, and P.A.G. Sabin (eds.), *The Second Punic War: A Reappraisal*, London: Institute of Classical Studies, 1996, pp. 81–95

——, 'Condottieri and Clansmen: Early Italian Raiding, Warfare and the State', Hopwood, K. (ed.), *Organized Crime in Antiquity*, Cardiff: Classical Press of Wales, 1999, pp. 97–127

——, 'Army and Battle during the Conquest of Italy (350–264 BC), in P. Erdkamp (ed.), *A Companion to the Roman Army*, Oxford: John Wiley & Sons (Blackwell Companions to the Ancient World), 2007, pp. 45–62

Rich, J.W., 'Warfare and the Army in Early Rome', in P. Erdkamp (ed.), *A Companion to the Roman Army*, Oxford: John Wiley & Sons (Blackwell Companions to the Ancient World), 2007, pp. 7–23

Richardson, A., *In Search of the Samnites: Adornment and Identity in Archaic Central Italy, 750–350* BC, Oxford: BAR Publishing (BAR International Series, 2550), 2016

Salmon, E.T., 'The Resumption of Hostilities after the Caudine Forks', *Transactions and Proceedings of the American Philological Association*, 87, 1956, pp. 98–108

——, 'Colonial Foundations during the Second Samnite War', *Classical Philology*, 58/4, 1963, pp. 235–38

——, *Samnium and the Samnites*, Cambridge: Cambridge University Press, 2010

Saulier, C., *L'Armée et la Guerre chez les Peoples Samnites (viie–ive s.)*, Paris, 1983

Schneider-Herrman, G., (ed. Herring, E.,), *The Samnites of the Fourth Century* BC: *As Depicted on Campanian Vases and in other Sources*, London: Institute of Classical Studies (Bulletin Supplement vol. 61), 1995

Scopacasa, R., *Ancient Samnium: Settlement, Culture, and Identity between History and Archaeology*, Oxford: Oxford University Press, 2015

Secunda, N., *Early Roman Armies*, Oxford: Osprey Publishing (Men-at-Arms 283), 1995

Small, A., 'The Use of Javelins in Central and South Italy in the 4th century BC', in D. Ridgeway, F.R. Serra Ridgeway, M. Pearce, E. Herring, R. Whitehouse and J. Wilkins (eds.), *Ancient Italy in its Mediterranean Setting: Studies in Honour of Ellen Macnamara*, London, 2000, pp. 223–34

Snodgrass, A.M., *Early Greek Armour and Weapons*, Edinburgh: Edinburgh University Press, 1965

Sommella, P., *Antichi Campi di Battaglia in Italia*, Roma: De Luca Editore (Quaderni dell'Istituto di Topografia Antica nell'Università di Roma 3), 1967

Tagliamonte, G., *I Sanniti: Caudini, Irpini, Pentri, Carricini, Frentani*, Milan: Longanesi, 1996

Terrenato, N., *The Early Roman Expansion into Italy: Elite Negotiations and Family Agendas*, Cambridge: Cambridge University Press, 2019

Tomczak, J., 'Roman Military Equipment in the 4th century BC: Pilum, Scutum and the Introduction of Manipular Tactics', *Folia Archaeologica*, 29, 2012, pp. 38–65

Toynbee, A.J., *Hannibal's Legacy: The Hannibalic War's Effect on Roman Life*, 2 vols, Oxford: Oxford University Press, 1965

Walbank, F.W., *A Historical Commentary on Polybios*, Vol. 1, Oxford: Clarendon Press, 1957

APPENDIX

Abbreviations of cited authors and works

App.	Appian	Oros.	Orosius
	B civ.	*Bellum civile*	Osc.	Oscan
	Sam.	*Σαυνιτική*	Ov.	Ovid
Arist.	Aristotle		*Fast.*	*Fasti*
	Pol.	*Πολιτκά*		*Met.*	*Metamorphoses*
Cic.	Cicero	Ph.	Philon
	Inv. rhet.	*De inventione rhetorica*		*Bel.*	*Belopeika*
	Leg. agr.	*De lege agraria*	Pl.	Pliny (the elder)
	Off.	*De officiis*		*HN*	*Naturalis historia*
	Orat.	*De oratore*	Polyb.	Polybios
	Sen.	*Cato Maior de Senectute*	P.Oxy. I 12	Oxyrhynchus Chronicle
	Tusc.	*Tusculanae Disputationes*	Plut.	Plutarch
Dio	Cassius Dio		*Cam.*	*Camillus*
Dio. Hal.	Dionysios of Halikarnassos		*Pyrr.*	*Pyrrhos*
	Ant. Rom.	*Antiquitates Romanae*	Ps.Skylax	Pseudo-Skylax
Diod. Sic.	Diodorus Siculus	Sall.	Sallust
Enn.	Ennius		*Cat.*	*Bellum Catiline*
	Ann.	*Annales*	Sil.	Silius Italicus
Etr.	Etruscan		*Pun.*	*Punica*
Eutr.	Flavius Eutropius	Strab.	Strabo
Fest.	Festus	Tac.	Tacitus
Flor.	Florus		*Hist.*	*Historiae*
Gell.	Aulus Gellius	Quint.	Quintinian
	NA	*Noctes Atticae*	Val. Max.	Valerius Maximus
Hom.	Homer	Var.	Varro
	Od.	*Odyssey*		*Ling.*	*De lingua Latina*
Hor.	Horace	Veg.	Vegetius
	Sat.	*Satirae*		*Mil.*	*De re militari*
ILS	H. Dessau (ed.), *Inscriptiones Latinae selectae*	Virg.	Virgil
	(Berlin, 1892–1916)		*Aen.*	*Aeneid*
Liv.	Livy		*G.*	*Georgics*
	Per.	*Periochae*	Zonar.	Zonaras
Luc.	Lucan			
	B civ.	*Bellum civile*		

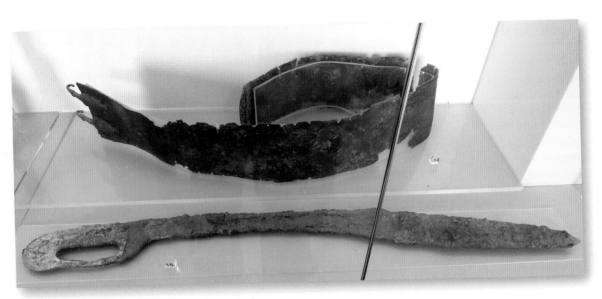

Oscan broad bronze belt and Greek *kopis* (Paestum, Museo Archeologico Nazionale di Paestum). The two large clasps are rather ornate, tapering into elongated arrowheads that curl around at their points, which fit into holes. Riveted attachment plates shaped like palmettes are used to attach these clasps to the belt. Manufactured from a hammered sheet of bronze, this was then stitched to leather lining by means of small drilled holes, which are clearly visible along both the top and bottom edges. The *kopis* was an iron leaf-shaped, single-edge slashing sword around 60cm in length. It was normally slung on a baldric over the right shoulder and served as a secondary weapon. A soldier's equipment could of course reflect his dexterity at looting the dead or prisoners, so that the more seasoned soldier probably boasted greater protection, an eclectic array of pieces and styles. (Dave & Margie Hill/Wikimedia Commons/CC-BY-SA-2.0)

Other abbreviations

c.	circa
fr.	fragment
ibid.	ibidem, in the same work
It.	Italian
Lat.	Latin
pl.	plural
q.v.	*quod vide*, see

Glossary

acies	line of battle
agmen	line of march
antilabê	handgrip of *aspis* (q.v.)
as (pl. *asses*)	small copper coin, worth 1/10th of *denarius*
aspis (pl. *aspides*)	'Argive shield' – soup-bowl shaped shield, 80–100cm diameter, held via an *antilabê* (q.v.) and a *porpax* (q.v.)
centurio (pl. *centuriones*)	officer in command of *centuria* (q.v.)
centuria (pl. *centuriae*)	administrative sub-unit of *manipulus* (q.v.)
clipeus (pl. *clipî*)	the Latin term for an *aspis* (q.v.)
cubit	ancient unit of measurement equal to the distance from the elbow bottom to the middle finger tip (444mm)
dilectus	'the pick' – muster at the beginning of each campaigning season
hasta (pl. *hastae*)	thrusting spear
imperium	coercive power of higher magistrates such as consul (q.v.)
knemides	greaves, bronze body armour for the lower legs
kopis	single-edged, heavy slashing-type sword shaped like a machete
La Tène	Iron Age culture named after site at La Tène, Lac de Neuchâtel
legio (pl. *legiones*)	'levy' – principal unit of Roman army
linothôrax	stiff linen corselet, which it is lighter and more flexible (but more expensive) than bronze body armour
manipulus (pl. *manipuli*)	'handful' – tactical sub-unit of *legio* (q.v.)
magister equitum	'master of horse' – deputy to a dictator
Montefortino	Gaulish necropolis site near Arcevia chosen as the eponym for a type of helmet most popular in Italy from 3rd to 1st centuries BC
pteruges	'feathers' – stiffened leather or linen fringing on corselet
optio (pl. *optiones*)	second-in-command of *centuria/turma* (q.v.)
pilum (pl. *pila*)	throwing weapon
porpax	armband of *aspis* (q.v.)
scutum (pl. *scuta*)	oval body shield
span	ancient unit of measurement equal to the distance across a man's outstretched hand (223mm), two spans equalling one cubit (q.v.)
triarios/triarii	'third-rank man' – veteran legionary forming *legio* (q.v.) third rank

INDEX

Note: page numbers in bold refer to illustrations, captions and plates.